Back-story

First Time Tales by the Stranger Next Door

SoLo X O Publishing
Boston, MA
2008

© 2008 by Jennifer H.R. Cutler

All rights reserved. No part of this publication my be reproduced or transmitted in any form or by any means, electronic or mechanical, including photocopy, recording, or any information storage and retrieval system, without permission in writing from Jennifer H.R. Cutler.

Requests for permission to make copies of any part of the work should be addressed to: jenniferhrcutler@gmail.com

First edition published by Lulu ® 2008
U.S. Copyright Office 2008
ISBN 978-0-6152-3983-5
Printed in the United States of America

Text set in Sylfaen – 12 pt
Cover Creation by Jacques G. Lopez

Photographs within this book provided by:
1. Dallas Bittle Digital Imaging: www.dallasbittle.com;
2. Amelia Cutler
3. Jennifer Lopez

Back-story:
First Time Tales by the Stranger Next Door

On Having Babies at Home in Rural Guatemala	*Margaret M. Kieffer*	P. 1
First Step on the Marathon Trail	*Jerry Lopez*	P. 9
An Episode in Florida	*Tonya Price*	P. 15
The First Time I Killed…On Stage	*Michael Conway*	P. 23
The Ladder	*Nathan Cutler*	P. 29
Descent from the Turret	*Jennifer Cutler*	P. 35
Ho B52	*Cecilia Unite*	P. 45
Alternative Class for First Timers	*Amanda Minaker*	P. 53
Elegy to my Marriage	*Cecilia Hutchinson*	P. 59
Potatoes for Ethiopia	*Shirley Pashley*	P. 63
Warning: This is not a Toy!	*Kim Jones*	P. 69
The Chalice	*Nathan Cutler*	P. 79
Small Town Girl	*Michelle Osmond*	P. 87
The Road Less Traveled By	*Patty Thille*	P. 95
Sometimes You Just Need To Jump In	*Anna Noble*	P. 103
Feet First	*Candace Clemens*	P. 111
Green	*Nathan Cutler*	P. 119
The Week I Died	*Chuck Duncan*	P. 125
A Writer's Confessional	*Jennifer Cutler*	P. 133

BACK-STORY

On Having Babies at Home in Rural Guatemala

Margaret M. Kieffer

In 1978 at the time of this story Margaret 'Peg' Kieffer was 38 years old and held a Ph.D. in cultural anthropology from the University of California at Irvine. She subsequently visited over 60 countries, experiencing many adventures prior to her death from cancer in March 2006. During her travels, her favorite site remained her home in Santiago Atitlan, Guatemala.

The baby was to be born in our own home by the lake in Santiago Atitlan with both my husband, Jerry and our American doctor friend who works in the town, John Emrich in attendance. John, knowing the ways of the world, had instructed Jerry in delivery techniques and cord tying just in case he was elsewhere occupied when the time arrived.

Jerry, who is also worldly wise, had painstaking planned and executed a system for communicating from the lake house, where I had retired two weeks before the due date, to Guatemala City, where Jerry continued his vigilant work at the embassy. The first phase of the system was a two-way radio link from my house and the house of the doctor a little less than a mile away. The radios installed we had set hours in the morning and evening for radio checks and general reporting of status. The second phase was through the local police radio. For this Jerry had to get special permission from the head of the Guatemala Police force. A special letter was written to introduce Dr. Emerich to the local police enlisting their aid in his communicating with Guatemala City and hence to my husband. John, of course, needed no introduction to the local police as his clinic was located in the same block just around the corner. Letters were also written from the Inspector General of the Police force to both Santiago Atitlan and Sololá where a radio message would be relayed to Guatemala City. In Guatemala City the police would use their regular communication channels to the Embassy. To complete the system, and as a back-up measure, an urgent telegram was to be sent at the same time to Jerry at the Embassy. (There is only one phone in Santiago located at the post/telegraph office which seldom is operational and then impossible to understand.)

At the lake house I was spending my time going through papers, cleaning up the house in preparation not only for the baby but guests from Florida who were due to arrive three days after the baby. Jerry was commuting every other day arriving between 11 and midnight to leave at 6:30 am on a three hour drive back to Guatemala City. After the first week we found that one of the radios was not recharging and Jerry took it back to the city to have it fixed. On Wednesday night he returned with the replacement. The doctor's wife Susan had been dropping by every evening between 6 and 7:00 pm, just to check as we had been without radio communication. Also, our faithful friend and caretaker, Salvador was at the house every day, but was free to spend his evening and nights with his family in town while there was someone at the house. In addition we had rented out the rancho in front of the house and there was a young couple who planned to stay two weeks. Our German Shepard Bazi, was also with me at the lake.

On Thursday, Jerry left early to return to the city. Salvador was working on carpentry tasks and I was finishing the hand waxing of the wood floors on the second level of the house. I had brought up our electric buffer from the city and wanted to finish before our erratic electricity went out as it had been doing on the previous days. It was well after day by the time I had finished. Salvador had left and was to purchase nails in town the following morning to replace our supply. Susan had not passed by as she normally did in the early evening. I fixed something to eat, fed Bazi and myself, and made my usual nightly mug of hot chocolate, to which I added the remainder of a bottle of rum in celebration of the completion of the floor waxing and a hard day's work. And so to bed.

At 11:30 that night I got up, as I often did at night, and headed for the bathroom thinking that I must be in the last stages of pregnancy as I was losing control. In reality, as I soon realized, the sac had broken and I was losing water.

The doctor when he had examined me on Sunday had said that he thought the baby might be a few weeks late. I had had no sensation of the baby having 'fallen' or moved down into the birth channel. His head was in the same place as it had been for the last few months. What could I do? Everyone had said that first-borns take a while in coming so I went back to bed. I stayed awake long enough to time the first few intervals, five minutes, then dozed off. By 4:30 am intermittent sleep was impossible and I was trying to figure all the ways I could get a message to the doctor. As the replacement radio was for the doctor's house, and as Susan had not come by in the evening, both radios were sitting on the floor in the bedroom. Oh well, I still had the couple in the rancho. I would write John a letter, and make a map of how to get to the doctor's house and at a decent hour, say 7:30, I would go down to the rancho, wake up its occupants, and ask them to do me the favour of calling the doctor.

At 5:30 I was up and after making another mug of hot chocolate, prepared the bedroom for the coming event. I brought in the small portable stove and boiled up the scissors and packing twine for 20 minutes, stripped and remade the bed starting with a shower curtain over the mattress, and cleared the bedroom of extraneous boxes. By 7:00 am I felt I could wait no longer so went down to the rancho to ask them to call the doctor. Half-way there, I realized no one was there – the padlock had been placed on the outside of the door. Friday morning, I guess that they had left at 3:00 AM to catch the bus to Sololá. Now what? Wait for Salvador – but Salvador was buying nails which meant he would have to wait in town until the store opened. As there is no predicting accurately when the store would open I could only imagine that it would be near or after 9:00. I undressed and went back to bed.

I found a position that was comfortable and settled down to wait for Salvador. At a little after 8:00, Bazi started barking. I figured that it was one of the locals either passing by within Bazi's view or someone looking for Salvador. After a minute or so of continued barking there was no choice I would have to go downstairs and see who it was. Up and to the task of getting dressed again, dressing being accomplished in the intervals between contractions. Such a simple thing should take so long—or at least it seemed to take a long time. And then down the stairs and to the front door. Lo, who cometh, the doctor's blessed wife ,Susan! My first words "Boy, am I happy to see you!" She had come by early because she missed the night before. Dr. John had to attend a dying patient and Susan had not had a car. And the good doctor, he had left this morning at 6:00 to go to another village in the highlands and was not expected back until the evening. Susan would go into town and get Ana Carlota, the 'nurse'-midwife who attended most of the deliveries at the hospital on the other side of town. Fortunately today was her day off. And off went Susan, to collect Ana and send Jerry the message to come, the baby was on its way. I went contentedly back to bed know that all would now be attended. All I had to do was keep relaxed and wait for Susan to return with Ana.

 Sometime later I realized that Salvador had come as I heard his attentions to morning chores. Shortly thereafter I heard Salvador in the corridor outside the bedroom. Someone from the city hall had come to request my presence in the judge's office downtown. According to local custom if there is a grievance one party goes to the judge who calls in the other party and they attempt to reach an understanding. We had been having a dispute over land boundaries near the lake and it was over this that my presence was requested. I told Sal through the closed door that I was sick and couldn't go. As someone had to heed the call he went in my place. Shortly thereafter Susan and Ana arrived.

 Ana had come thinking that she would just check on my progress, then come back later when she figured it would be time. Fooled her! I had just been waiting for her to come.

 And what of the attempts to reach Jerry? Susan had first gone to the local police station only to find that the police radio was not functioning. Next she had gone to the telegraph office. There she found that the one telegrapher had been called to Sololá for a meeting and was not expected to return until evening. She left the telegraph message anyway and went to the Health Clinic where they had set up a CB radio link with the clinic in Sololá. Unfortunately during the day there is a lot of static over the air and other than being able to identify the message as originating in Santiago nothing else got through. She asked that they send the message with their normal evening transmission. She had next gone to the local church which has an American padre on its staff. Father Francisco volunteered to drive the

10 miles of potted dirt road to send the telegraphy message from the adjacent town. In the meantime he had a few chores to do.

Back at the lake house the baby was attempting to emerge from an orifice somewhat smaller than its head. After a 40 minute confrontation the orifice conceded and Jacques Gerard opened his eyes and his mouth and cried his way into the world. Ana said "It's a boy!" and proceeded to rest; after all, in Guatemala, if you don't produce a son, you have accomplished nothing. Ana tied the cord with the packing string and cut it with the home sterilized scissors; after all she had not intended to stay after the initial examination and didn't have an obstetric pack with her.

We then sat around and chatted for three hours waiting for the placenta which was just about as reluctant to appear as was Jacques. Afterward Susan buried the same, fertilizing one of our flowering shrubs and later we drank a cup of warm champagne. The baby being five days early had preceded the chilling of the bottle. Ana went into town to see if the doctor at the health center could come to put in the stitches. He was occupied with the stitching of the head of an Indian woman and had a full waiting room. Ana came back with the necessities and did the sewing while I read aloud from a Gorgetta Heyer novel, Cousin Kate. By now it was early evening and Ana went home while Susan collected some things from her house, left the doctor a note and came back to spend the night.

Shortly after 11:00 PM Bazi started to bark and I waited a few moments to see if Susan was getting up. No sound from her room so I threw on a robe and went downstairs to let Jerry in. He had received a message at the Embassy at 7:00 that evening. Apparently the radio at the Health Clinic succeeded in getting through to Sololá and hence to Guatemala City. The telegram arrived in Guatemala the following day. The good padre had not gone to the next town to send the telegram as by the time he was ready to go the baby had already arrived. So here was the new father probably just as relieved to arrive after the fact as he was sorry to have missed it. Ten minutes later there is another knock on the downstairs door and Doctor John arrives with a bag and a book already to spend the night with the expectant mother. Susan's note just said that she was at the house with me and nothing about the baby having arrived. We all drank a glass of now chilled champagne, finishing the bottle. John and Susan then left for home amongst best wishes and many thanks. I'm convinced that each of us that night went to sleep feeling that we had accomplished a good day's work.

First Step on the Marathon Trail

Jerry Lopez

Jerry Lopez is a retired US Army officer and Special Agent, Diplomatic Security Service, U.S. Department of State. Since his initial Bangkok marathon, he has completed 76 marathons, including two 50-mile ultra-marathons and is a member of the Seven Continents Club, having done a marathon on every continent.

Where's the hoopla! Where are the cheering spectators!! What am I doing at this crazy hour at 3:30AM!!!

My taxi has just dropped me off at the Start Assembly area for the Bangkok Marathon on this hot and humid morning of November 23, 1997. I had visions of masses of energetic spectators amidst a gaily decorated start line. Instead, I find the runners waiting under an overpass, a simple Start banner, and very few spectators. I am feeling even more anxious as all the Thai runners appear to be exemplars of fitness and youth. At 52 years and 200 pounds, I am feeling age and weight-challenged. Doubt floods my mind as I wonder if I can really last the 26.2 miles in this adverse climate. There are relatively few foreigners amongst the runners. Should I just drop out now and do an easier first marathon in a more agreeable and runner-friendly ambience??

My anxiety level is peaking as we walk to the start line on the freeway. I feel on the verge of insanity as the 4:30 AM start time nears. Have I really trained sufficiently? Many similarly nervous runners are using the toilets in this remaining time. We can all clearly feel the increasing tension and adrenalin among us. A nearby runner candidly tells me that he is frightened at the thought of running his first marathon. I respond that he will be fine and that I will see him at the Finish line. My state of ignorance makes my words more credible.

The starting horn sounds and most of us scream to release stress. We all surge into the darkness, do a short loop, pass by the starting area again, and then we continue on the freeway. This year's marathon route consists of freeways and asphalt streets. There are no scenic landmarks or views and no cheering spectators, but there is ample heat, humidity, and pollution. Once the sun rises at about 6:20 AM, the temperature soars into the 80's. Shade is an infrequent commodity, so most of the time I feel like a French fry on a steaming skillet.

Runners begin dropping out from dehydration and severe chaffing in the groin area. There are very few female runners, possibly due to the absence of any toilets on the route. I am at the back of the pack and fixate on just finishing within the six hour time limit. The Thai runners are absolutely great! Although language between us is very limited to non-existent, many Thais are clearly happy to see a foreigner, especially an older and grey-haired one, in this race. They keep encouraging me with warm smiles, basic words, and thumbs-up gestures.

By 8:30AM, the heat and humidity are steaming from the asphalt. It's a clear sky so the sun feels intense. The stronger runners are considerably ahead of us slower ones who are being decimated. The ambulances and medical teams are quite busy. This race has become a mental exercise to stay focused on just finishing, regardless of time. Willpower is the only recourse. For nearly five miles, I keep company with two older Thais, probably in their 60's, as we jog, walk, and shuffle along. Their mutual support and courage to keep going is moving. But in the end, they falter and have to stop. I reluctantly wave farewell and find virtually no other runners with me this far back in the pack.

Whether I finish or not, I have had incredible insights in how I deal with intense fatigue and stress. Quite often the body has been screaming to stop with the mind momentarily concurring. Facing these strong realities of hopelessness and frustration, I have to summon my inner positive spirit, disregard the pain, and will myself to conquer this marathon dragon.

Somehow, I make it to the final freeway segment. At a quarter mile from the Finish line, I have five minutes remaining before the six hour time limit. Except for a Thai about 100 feet ahead, there is on one else left on the field. Suddenly, this Thai falters and falls exhausted to the ground to rest. In the distance, I can hear the officials and a few spectators clapping and yelling encouragement to beat the time limit. The last energy reserves respond, and I cross the Finish line as the clock strikes 6 hours! I am the last official finisher and receive the Finisher's medal in a mixed state of euphoria and exhaustion.

I had not done anything this physically and mentally intense since Army Officer Candidate School twenty-seven years earlier. I am hooked on marathons! It's impossible to run a marathon and be emotionally neutral. You either never want to run another marathon or you can't wait for the next one. For me as a slow runner, doing a marathon is an incredibly intense experience in which I feel very strong bonds of camaraderie with the other runners, experience intense surges of energy and well-being, and feel inspired from seeing so many handicapped or exhausted runners overcome adversity through sheer determination.

After completing 75 marathons on all seven continents, the thrill and adrenalin rush still remain. Onward to the next marathon!!

An Episode in Florida

Tonya Price

Tonya believes that dealing with a mentally ill parent has made her stronger and able to face any difficult situation with ease. She currently lives in Ottawa and is enjoying a successful career as a public servant. She hopes that the perception and treatment of mental illness will continue to improve.

When I was about 10 years old my family decided to spend the winter in Florida. Oh how lovely it was. We drove down the east coast of the USA in our big emerald green Cadillac. With every mile we ventured south the weather got warmer and we were excited about our final destination: Daytona Beach. We saw many interesting landmarks and had the opportunity to spend time with our friends in beautiful Savannah, Georgia. I was excited for new experiences. I was also nervous with so many uncertainties, but I knew deep down that everything would work out and I felt reassured, as I always had been with my parents and my brother. Yet there was something I didn't know. Something my Mom had in the back of her mind and something that had always made my Dad the life of the party.

Florida was such a nice change from cold Canada, especially in the middle of the winter. It was warm, carefree, and peaceful. We had lots of fun in the beginning. The condo we lived in was beautiful and luxurious. Our living conditions were idyllic as compared with what they had been at home where we lived outside of the city in a house in various stages of renovation. My Dad was always changing things and didn't like sitting still. Florida offered new experiences, resort-like living conditions, and the potential for several memorable and enjoyable months.

My Dad got a job at a local bar. We had an underground bar at home for years so this is what my Dad knew and it was a natural choice for employment. He did fine from the beginning and got along well with the owners; he found his niche and was enjoying the work. Maybe he was enjoying it too much.

Mickey Gilley was having a show at the bar one night and Dad was really excited about seeing him perform. I remember the evening of the show because I had gone to the bar with Mom and Dad. It seemed weird to be inside the bar, yet I don't remember it lasting much longer than a few minutes; I think we dropped Dad off and then went home. I do remember that the bar had a western theme complete with a mechanical bull which I got to sit on. I felt good about the whole event.

Apparently Dad felt pretty good too, a little too good in fact. After so many years it is hard to know how conscious he was of what he was doing or why he did what he did. Who knows if he had too much to drink or if he had taken something else? We will never know what drove him to do the things he did that night.

My Mom knew something was up. She always knew. She seemed nervous and ill at ease that night. She was restless and probably wanted to be at home, in a familiar and safe environment. Years later, I have developed the same intuition and I can tell when Dad is manic, even from a thousand kilometers away. The night of Mickey Gilley's show was the last blissful night in Florida and I was totally unaware of the impending impact that mental illness was about to have on the rest of my life.

My brother and I slept well that night and we didn't know anything was wrong until the next morning. We were at the condo when we got the call. We rushed to the hospital to see if Dad was ok and to find out what had happened. It was terrifying and we didn't know exactly what to expect. The hospital smelled gross and it was so bright and real.

I remember what Dad looked like: so weak and vulnerable. He was obviously injured. He was sedated due to his mental illness and due to the trauma he had caused to his body. We were all in a state of shock and his apparent disability coupled with all the additional responsibilities my Mom now had to deal with made us very scared. Thankfully we had purchased health insurance, but the bureaucracy related to having a life threatening injury in another country was an experience for which my Mom was ill prepared and loath to deal with.

The events of that fateful night became clearer in the following days. We found out he left the bar very late at night and went walking towards the ocean. He had decided to go swimming, with his clothes on. Afterwards his belt buckle was green due to the oxidization of the salt water, which was a key clue as to how the night unfolded. After the swim in the ocean he was unsatisfied and he kept walking down the beach. He ended up at one of the big waterfront hotels. He walked up to the pool and seemingly without hesitation dove in, head first into the deep end. This would have been fine except for the fact there was no water in the pool; it was virtually empty with only a little skiff of dirty water left in the deep end. He was lucky to be alive.

My Dad came home after only a few days in hospital. He had a plaster cast on his nose and several stitched up gashes on his forehead and chin. Poor Dad, he was so sore and needed to rest and recover. I don't remember having much contact with him for the first few days. He was obviously injured and he smelt weird. I found him scary to look at and as I was unsure how to deal with him, I stayed out of his room. In hindsight I can now see that staying away from him when he is ill has become my coping mechanism. I didn't know how to deal with his injuries or his mental illness at that time and despite years of trying I still don't.

My Mom was left to take care of everything. She had no support system and she had to be the strong, capable one. Without my Dad working, my Mom needed to find a job and it wasn't long before she was working at the local diner. She scraped together enough resources to get us an apartment and all the while tried to maintain a sense of normalcy for my brother and me. We visited the beach regularly, we spent a day at Disney World, and the three of us shared many fun experiences, always without my Dad.

The apartment that my Mom found for us was less than optimal. It was a 'fixer-upper' that needed some pretty serious renovations. I don't think it had been lived in for quite a while but my Dad vowed to do the necessary work on it once he recovered from the accident. Until he recovered, however, our living conditions were not the finest. There were mice in the apartment and other bugs and vermin that made my Mom fearful for the health and safety of her children; yet, my brother and I were seemingly unaware and saw it as a rustic house that was teeming with potential.

The apartment was really the back section of what was probably at one time a very beautiful house. It was only a few blocks from the beach with a circular driveway and fruit trees in the backyard. Time and coastal weather had dirtied the facade and left the house looking worn and in need of attention. The fruit trees in the backyard were either overgrown or dead. The yard looked prickly and menacing as if it had forgotten what it felt like to have children playing in it and exploring its corners. We did lots of exploring in the first few days of living at the Kirkwood House and in the corners of the yard we found cute little lizards. My brother loved to pick them up and show them to me. The vegetation in the yard was so different from what we were used to in our northern climate and we had lots of fun discovering new plants and crawling creatures.

The front part of the house was occupied by two very old ladies and their skinny, sickly dog. I remember the dog clearly. He was so thin you could clearly see his spine and he had an illness that made him loose patches of fur leaving the sores on his skin exposed. Despite his poor health he was still friendly and fit well with the general feel of the house; however, as he really was pretty gross we tried to avoid the front part of the house and stayed in our backyard. It seemed safer.

We had gotten a good deal on the rent so it was hard to complain about the conditions. We all pitched in to clean up the apartment; opening the windows to let in the warm Florida sun, buying cheap furniture, and getting into the rhythm of southern life. The vermin quickly disappeared and my Mom became more at ease with the whole situation. My Dad's mania was getting better too. I suppose that diving into a pool with no water would definitely jar your mood and quickly bring you back to reality. It was probably hard for him too, but I think he was mostly oblivious for the first while. Slowly he reintegrated into our lives and began the renovations. Every day when my brother and I came home from school there were improvements to our living conditions.

Despite all of the new and exciting experiences in Florida, my memories have always been overshadowed by Dad's mania. His first manic episode was so overwhelming to me. So much happened in a short period of time and because we were so insular, my immediate family was inevitably and profoundly affected. There was nowhere to go and nowhere for us to escape, so we had to deal with Dad and the implications of his disease.

Since then, I have experienced my Dad's mania so many times that the episodes just blur together into one horrible experience. Yet, it is possible to pick out isolated incidents, the ones that have caused me the most stress and the most traumas. His manic episodes have become predictable and cyclic. If only they were a positive experience, it would be reassuring for something in life to be so reliable. Yet that is not the case; my Dad's mania has been devastating. The episodes I haven't witnessed firsthand, I have had to deal with through the trauma my Mom and my brother have experienced. Many times since I have moved away from home I have been grateful for the distance. But after having him show up on my doorstep unannounced numerous times, I have learnt that even distance cannot protect me or the people in my life from his illness.

He has never been successfully treated for his disease so I have had to deal with one or two manic episodes every year, each one lasting between one to three months. He has caused so many problems for my family. He has verbally abused us so often that we consider it normal; he has broken many windows; destroyed vehicles; spend time in jail and in mental institutions; and he has lost his driver's license so many times that I have lost count. I have undergone trauma, terror, and many frustrations. I have had my life thrown upside down by his craziness and I am always left wondering when the next manic episode will happen. Every time he calls I analyze his voice and his words as I try to discern if he is fine or heading towards mania. Once the mania subsides he is left remorseful and depressed. He can't believe that he has spent so much money and destroyed things that were important to him. He has to rebuild his home, his relationships, and his credit, only to have everything he cares about destroyed a few months later. Yet there must be something he enjoys, the highs are very high and feeling like 'the chosen one' must have an allure. The costs have been enormous to him and to us, yet the bipolar disorder persists, and my desire for normalcy has never been attained.

  Despite everything I still love him and he is my one and only Dad. I have taught him about his illness and tried so hard to get him to take medication or undergo some sort of treatment, but always without success. I only want for him to have a happy, peaceful life. Also for purely selfish reasons I don't want to have to deal with the mania ever again. It would be nice to say that the first time dealing with a manic episode was the worst time but it wasn't. In addition to the aforementioned property damages, the damage to our family has been devastating as well. My brother suffered for many years from a terrible drug addiction and I still have yet to uncover the traumas I have experienced. My mom continues to suffer his wrath and harassment despite having left him many years ago.

  My dad is now 74 years old and while he is physically in great shape he has never given the same care to his mental health. When he is good, he is very good, but when he is bad, he is horrid. Recently he told me he wanted to swim with dolphins so I thought, why not and we planned a vacation to Florida. I was hoping for a trip to finally heal the wounds that continue to haunt me from our first trip to Florida. After buying airplane tickets, making reservations, and planning excursions, all had to be cancelled because the mania returned once again. I was unwilling to relive that terrible trip south and dealing with the disappointment was easier than dealing with his mania. I think this was a last ditch effort to have a 'normal' relationship with my father, but it was not meant to be. His illness ensures that he is not normal; it also makes certain that I cannot have a normal father/daughter relationship with him. I will continue to grieve this realization and continue to dream about what could have been. My father has a mental illness and he won't be getting better.

The First Time I Killed...On Stage.

Michael J. Conway

Michael is a freelance writer for major magazine publishers. Reading classic short stories spurred his passion for literature. His creativity was instigated during periods of isolation when he was morbidly obese. He reports, "I isolate no more." Residing in Massachusetts with his family, he can be reached at mjcon6@msn.com.

The very first time I attempted stand-up comedy was at the old *Catch A Rising Star* in Harvard Square, Cambridge, Massachusetts. It was so long ago I can't even remember the year - maybe '88 or '89. What I do remember, vividly, was that I killed.

The months prior I had become very tired and bored with my monstrous 440 pound-ish body and mind. I was employed at a *Casual Male Big & Tall* in Saugus. Part-time, I was advisor to wives of other fat men as to what color would look good on Leo, or the like, back at the homestead. Occasionally one of these wives would become perturbed when 6x sweatpants were only available in the shade of my boss's Pontiac out in the lot, flat black.

"Do you have any of these in blue out back?" the hag would crazily ask.

"Let me check."

I would saunter in a swaying gait, unintentionally hip checking racks of shirts, while exiting the valley of oversized clothing. Out back, I would start eating my roast beef sandwich while fantasizing of robbing the safe of the gregarious garmented district.

Eventually I would return to Doris or the like, "Sorry, we don't have the 6x in blue. We only have the black."

"How about socks? Charlie's ankles swell. Will these ones be big enough? He's about your size."

So I would be forced to think of myself in the future, a few decades or so. What will my ankles be like then? I thought to myself. Fuck Doris I would silently reply. Charlie too!

"I think we have something out back," and I returned to my roast beef.

So as you can see, with this mind set and rogue of social characters, and my own swelling ankles, I decided to enter an open mike night that was advertised in a Boston magazine. One had to show up on Monday nights, and show up on Monday nights, and show up on Monday nights. Sign up on the waitlist, on the waitlist, on the waitlist. More or less, it was kind of kiss the club managers ass for a month or two. Then my day came.

I drove my battleship car down Memorial Drive with my cousin Scott riding shotgun. It was hot out and my '78 Chevy something or another was beginning to sweat from her nose. A speeding Town Car nearly clipped us. Only a few miles to go.

Scott and I arrived on J.F.K. Boulevard and backed the Chevy into a spot leaving my bumper kissing cars at the front and stern. Patrons of an outdoor restaurant stared with fear one dons in the presence of a serial killer. The college town was hopping, my fear of the public due to obesity was paralyzing, but I would not be deterred. With a green garbage bag under my arm, I climbed the cobblestone sidewalk with my partner in crime until we finally descended the stairwell to the basement club known as "*Catch*."

Performing that night between amateur acts was Louis C.K., who went on to write for national TV comedians, and Frank Santorelli who later became a mobster on the Sopranos. But the individual I remember most was a guy in the bathroom. Appearing later, he was practicing his act in the mirror. He had a neurological disorder, of which I can not recall, and his jokes were centered on his disability. My jokes were centered on my fatness. I was number 6 or 7 out of 9 or 10 to go up that night. I was nervous, scared shit. I had a shot of Jack Daniels, felt the buzz, leaned against a stool, and promised myself never to drink before my act again.

The first three comedians did well then neurological guy came up and bombed. Scott and I went into a back room/ closet type of deal to change. In the green garbage bag was a pair of size 78 nylon brown pants, a 5x t-shirt, and suspenders all bought at employee's discount at the *Casual Male*. There was also a hula hoop sliced at one point so to manipulate though the pants like a belt. We exited the closet just prior to being introduced to the stage.

"I don't know what to say about this guy, but I think you're goin' to like him. Please welcome Mike Connwaaaaay."

I waddled to the stage not knowing if I would be able to speak because of the overwhelming fear. I shook the host's hand, heard the deafening silence, and then was amazed by the blinding stage lights that allowed limited sight of the first few rows. Scott could have been in Connecticut now for all I could discern.

A few chuckles, me scared shit, the deafening silence, I began, "I don't care if I suck...I figure if I bomb... you might throw some food."

The response was more than overwhelming. I laughed myself. I was killing. It was going great. Awesome, awesome, awesome. After he consumed a probable half dozen beers, the promised heckler appeared. With alcohol courage he blurted something or another aloud. The crowd turned toward him like Romans to Caesar.

I responded, "You're just jealous because I have bigger tits than your wife." Again the deafening applause. I was Caligula.

"Only five minutes," the club manager had allotted all the comics prior to the show.

After six minutes I reported to the crowd, "I can't do this anymore," and proceeded to disrobe my outer garment. When I was down to my true 64 inch pants I said, "You guys really thought I was fat?"

Killed.

I went into a parody of Sinatra singing, 'I gained it my way,' told one more fat joke, then thanked the crowd. It was more than eight minutes of heaven. While the crowd was astounded, the club manager let me know with a scowl that I went beyond my five minutes. Fuck 'im, I thought.

I went on to other open mike nights and eventually became an opening act at clubs in and around Boston. Along the way I met various personalities like Larry Reppucci, Jim Lauletta, Billy Martin and Tony V., all of which I found endearing. I often see old fellow comics on TV like Joe Rogan from *Fear Factor/ U.F.C.* My favorite comedians were Eddie Brill and D.J. Hazard.

It is almost twenty years later. Several months ago I returned to the stage to an open mike night. At a pub in Somerville, as the crowd stared and my first joke was told, the Red Line was heard off in the distance. Simply put, I bombed.

Recently I got married and inherited a beautiful wife and four awesome stepsons, and feed my Italian Greyhound whipped cream just because. I battle an ongoing worsening dilemma of mild cerebral palsy yet find time to bike for kids with cancer. I've found humor helpful throughout. I tell my wife, "I never walked like this until I laid eyes on you." I told my stepson's girlfriend I was shot in the face by organized crime.

Ten years ago I had gastric bypass surgery after superseding 500 pounds. I now weigh 201. Occasionally over the years someone would ask me, "What happened with your skin after you lost the weight?" I gently inform them I had plastic surgery and made a calzone.

I work full-time at FedEx and do some freelance writing for major publications. Writing is the only creative form I've found as enjoyable as performing, at times on lonely nights, on the stages in Boston and her surroundings, back in the '80's and '90s when I often killed.

The Ladder

Nathan Cutler

Nathan Hartley Cutler was born in Ramea, a fishing community off the coast of Newfoundland. Nathan and his twin brother were born in the family home's sitting room by the local mid-wife just two months after Newfoundland became the tenth Canadian province. He currently resides in New Brunswick, Canada.

The faint smell of smoke still clung to my hands and hair. In my mind's eye I still saw the orange and gold flames leaping skyward, its flankers and hot cinders carried by a slight breeze out over the sea. The scent of roasted potatoes still lingered in my nose. My teacher broke my wandering as he lay down his notes. "Class dismissed."

On our way out of the classroom, the teacher reminded everyone the assignment on Ernest Hemmingway was due by Friday. The assignment had been given a week ago, but time had not permitted me to even think on the subject. All my energy, like the rest of my friends, had gone into collecting things: tree branches, wooden crates, and old tires; in essence anything that could burn.

It had been the lead up to Guy Fawkes Night, Nov 5th, commonly called Bonfire Night. This was a tradition that had gone back over the generations to the old country and continued on; the one night each year we could stay out late with the other members of our community and watch the Bonfire burn and roast potatoes. We immersed ourselves into collecting anything from around town that wasn't secured down to throw into the fire. The unspoken code known by everyone was that if 'things' were left outside, then it was fair game to be used as fuel.

Walking home now, the day after, I was astutely aware of the last item several friends, my brother, and I had taken late into the night and thrown onto the Bonfire. No doubt the major coupe of the evening! As I drew closer to Aunt May's house, which was just a stones throw from ours, I became keenly aware that I had to pass directly in front of the garden where the ladder had rested for the last few weeks. There was no question that it had been the object of all our desires and with wishful thinking all hoped that Aunt May would not put away the ladder for safe keeping. The resting place of the dry wooden ladder was in easy access just waiting to be swooped upon by the group of us especially under the cover of night.

Sure enough the ladder had lay in full view right up to Bonfire Night. By the time the roaring fire had begun to die down, we boys knew exactly the thing that would rekindle the flames and so we quietly stole into the old lady's garden. Without a sound, we took the ladder putting it to capital use as it prolonged the fire and extended our fun late into the cool autumn evening.

The ladder was about twelve feet long, made of wood and painted grey and as I walked home from school, passing the spot where it once rested, I felt a rush of guilt as this was the first time I had actually stolen anything. Dismissing the feeling was a much weightier task than I had anticipated.

Our neighbor, referred to as Aunt May by everyone, was a bit of a recluse and was seldom seen around town. She attended only to her own business, rarely visiting people in our little town. My faint hope now was that she wouldn't miss the ladder from her garden. She didn't need it anyway, I reasoned. What would she do with it? Surely she would not suspect my friends and I of anything untoward as we pretty well never did anything to cause grief in our community. We were good kids, angelic almost.

Anyway, it should have been stored away safely. It was a high risk for the fire so she was stupid in leaving it outdoors on Bonfire Night, I mused. I tried to smile, but it was a vain attempt at redemption. The twang of guilt and a foreboding mood remained as I tried to dismiss my thoughts about the ladder all the while attempting to turn to the English assignment the teacher was trying to interest us in for the past week: it had something to do with justice.

The smell of freshly baked bread caught my nose as I opened the gate onto the small path leading to our house. Hmmm…I wonder what mom has for supper.

But before I opened the door onto the kitchen I knew by the low drone of adult conversation drifting in mono-tone onto the porch that we had company. I could also sense it was serious as I couldn't hear my brother or sisters; this meant they were either out or had taken refuge in the sitting room or their bedrooms. Whatever was up? I pushed open the door.

"You know Aunt May from next door," said my dad.

I nodded, speechless. Aunt May was looking very concerned and by all appearances on a mission. My parents carried on their conversation as I slowly crossed the kitchen to get a drink from the fridge, trying ever so hard to appear cool and non-guilty. I wanted so much to disappear, but the only thought I had was to remain calm and try to hold in the great urge to wet my pants.

Aunt May stood up to leave.

"Not to worry," said Dad. "I will replace it."

I dreaded sitting down for supper. I knew my parents were going to be upset and I would have to be punished; they would be hurt and dismayed I had stolen the ladder from Aunt May. It was the first time I had committed such a deed and now I would burn in hell, a place as hot I'm sure as Aunt May's ladder last night.

All was quiet as the meal started. I waited with baited breath for the bomb to drop. I didn't have to wait long.

"Too bad Aunt May feels so upset," said Dad.

I felt my face turn red, water pooling near the ridge of my eyelids. With a loss of appetite, a desperate prayer silently went up to all the Saints. Surely my parents could see the guilt written all over me.

"I told her not to worry about my ladder," continued Dad. "I can always buy a new one."

Words can not describe the warm wave of relief that engulfed me: Aunt May had no idea who had stolen the ladder. In a second my elation at not being found out dissipated like smoke as a cold dampness took possession of my hands and a radiant heat moved from my chin up to my brow. Just as the flames last night consumed the ladder now my absolute horror consumed me as I realized I had unwitting stolen my dad's ladder; the same one Aunt May had borrowed several weeks earlier. I finished my meal in silence as my teacher's lesson on poetic justice earlier today struck home.

Descent from the Turret

Jennifer Cutler

Jennifer has a Masters in International Development from Saint Mary's University, Halifax, Nova Scotia, attained in part by thesis research conducted in India. She loves to explore new places and ways of thinking; she currently lives in the U.S. and has visited forty-two of fifty states.

I spent my first two months in India baffled and frustrated. My first major solo expedition overseas, I secured a spot as a visiting resident at a fairly reputable university that focused on development issues. Two broken promises by the administration on the day of my arrival: no one to meet me at the airport and no accommodations when I actually did find the campus set the tone. Within two weeks, I contracted scabies from my overpriced and questionable mattress and was forced into a reluctant tolerance of sharing my living quarters with mutant size ants, slugs, cockroaches, and mosquitoes. Disillusionment was born.

The formidably hot day-lit hours were tailed by wild rain storms. Descending from the Atlantic region of Canada, I wilted under the Indian heat; at home I came alive in the cool autumn winds and the crisp winter air. The only food readily available at the cafeteria was the local specialty: mushy purple rice stirred with hot curry served three times a day. Utensils not included. As a visitor, I was not permitted access to the student's internet lab, a rule strictly enforced, so I was obliged to rouse myself from sleep to embark on post-midnight clandestine missions to fight the maddeningly slow internet connection. I had no access to a phone either. Requests to bend these rules were formally denied; a concept foreign to me: weren't guests supposed to be treated with grace and respect? I grew bitter of the administration as I became certain I represented nothing more to them than a westerner with money. The students were friendly enough, but I was an outsider, a foreigner, and by default, a Christian. The one Indian Christian girl in residence was ostracized by the Hindu students so I didn't have a prayer when it came to social inclusion.

Dirt roads and dust storms, daily sightings of animal neglect, whisperings of how residents of the Muslim neighborhood down the street despised all westerners, impossible to decipher body language, and dismay at the draconian bureaucratic apparatus around each corner wore me down at an alarming rate. I bit my tongue at public displays of nose-cleaning which included hawking, sniffing, blowing, and detaching with the left hand, and my desperation at the bleak poverty everywhere created a new me: a head-shaking loner who just wanted to bury her head from the utter rawness of life.

On weekends, I traveled by local bus to seaside destinations: the Arabian Sea to the west, the Bay of Bengal to the east, and the Indian Ocean directly to my south.

One Saturday morning, I embarked on the bus to Varkala, a hidden paradise on the Arabian Sea. Ignoring the usual unflinching stares, I squeezed to the back of the bus to find standing room only in the designated section for women. The dust rose from the dirt road as we barreled through rudimentary construction sites littered with working woman and children. Past Mahatma Gandhi hospital and into the country side, the bus convulsed stopping and starting in spontaneously created lanes of traffic. We passed through a dozen villages buried in the jungle just a few miles from the coastline. Eventually the bus emptied enough to leave me a seat and the window's metal bars to hang onto.

At the next stop, a stooped white haired lady shuffled onto the bus and behind her, appeared *the man*.

He wasn't the first local man I had seen with deformities. A few miles from my school, a middle-aged man made his living selling good-luck pendants spread out on an old towel alongside the congested street. He walked on all fours, did business that way, his back hunched, and his hands wearing the same style of worn sandals as on his feet. One of the construction workers at the school had a foot so twisted, he walked on the side of it, and another man who owned a chai-cart by the hospital had a limp arm, stretched out as though the elastic band inside had snapped.

But the man climbing onto the bus was a leper and quite definitely the most repulsive human I'd ever seen. Hands down. Fleshy bubbles the size of grapes hung from his face, his ears, his neck, and shoulders. He peered from underneath a mass of bushy dark hair. The pressure of heavy boils pushed his right eye into a narrow squint, his left eye as malleable as a soft boiled egg with its end chopped off.

He hobbled along the aisle swinging his head from side to side in order to stare at the passengers. Emitting a low moan, he begged in typical Indian style by tapping his fingers to his lips. Each digit was abnormally short, ending in crumbly toothpicks of skin. He stopped halfway down the aisle, his groans ceasing. He gripped either side of his unbuttoned filthy pink dress shirt and ripped it open.

I instinctively shied pressing my sweaty skin against the hot plastic seat. The leper's torso was covered in what looked like half-filled water balloons of skin giving him the appearance of multiple sagging breasts. Intermixed with these were smaller loose sacs of flesh. The driver barked something at him once, then again, and the leper scowled. He turned from his audience hobbling down the metal steps back onto the dirt road. The bus driver slammed his foot on the gas, and we barreled away from the leper leaving him in a cloud of dust.

I looked back at him through the glassless window. This man had no chance of a livelihood, his deformities too much even for the typical karma-noting Indian. And the agony of India skinned another layer of hope and optimism from my heavy heart.

~~~~~~~~~

After the weekend, I returned to the sanctuary of my school. Leafy and tree-covered, cool and quiet, it was guarded by a league of local men and a high stone wall. A microcosm of India: upper caste students working towards Masters Degrees and PhDs strolled in unisex groups past lower caste men lugging bricks and cement piled high on their shoulders and heads. Literally back-breaking labour. These same men made the bricks with a rudimentary machine as others shoveled clay and sand from a small pit at the back of the campus. The construction worker's lots were caste at birth. Men in their early twenties worked side by side with their future: eighty year olds whose wrinkly brown skins were wrapped in no more than loose sarongs and turbans.

I spent many afternoons in the school's library, an impressive building made of red stone. A set of narrow winding stairs led upwards to a secluded and covered turret rooftop. Here atop the hundreds of twisting stairs was a panoramic view of endless jungle stopping only at the sparkling ocean to the south. All around me, birds cawed in the thick tree tops and the jungle's most secretive creature the great tiger snored under the large canopies of teardrop leaves.

One afternoon after reading a series of articles from my rooftop study, I descended from the turret. The sky was the color seen mostly in paintings. A fiery orange sun large on the horizon elevated the deep red and purple skies to cover the entire world. A hazy light reflected on the trees and flowers, the buildings, and the hundreds of circling dragonflies to create a living painting of deep, dark tones. This was my favorite time of day. Lasting only half a hour or so, the palm trees became a violent green in the twilit light and the world stood still as though dozing, occasional bird peeps trickling from the trees. And everything seemed, if just for a moment, to be exactly how it is was meant to be.

I strolled along the winding road snaking past the administration buildings, laboratories, cafeteria, male residence, and headed towards the women's residence. Around the corner a hundred feet ahead of me by the badminton courts, the evening's peace was broken by a small commotion. Several of the university's higher level administrators had gathered around an auto-rickshaw. The administrators were all simultaneously gesturing with great animation while speaking in Malayalam, the local language, at a volume that indicated some sort of agitation. The driver was frantically pointing into the ditch that ran along the narrow road.

I slowed my pace attempting to interpret the body language: all the men were concerned, the three higher-caste and usually disinterested administrators were treating this exchange with the rickshaw driver with a mixture of arrogance and reluctant attention as though they couldn't ignore whatever information with which the driver had interrupted them.

I saw another student, whom I had played the occasional badminton game, approaching.

"What's going on, Ahmed?"

"The driver saw a cobra cross the street. It went down into that ditch." He pointed at the mess of bramble and knee-high yellowing grass.

I scurried back a few steps. "A cobra? Really? Um, so what are they going to do?" I stared into the field of thick brush. Cut regularly by machete-wielding gardeners, this all day affair was seemingly pointless as each week the grass appeared to grow back thicker and lusher, an unstoppable force of nature. Half way between where Ahmed and I stood and the library on the far end of the field were three deep stone wells used as the campus garbage dump. "You think it's going for the rodents in the well?"

"Perhaps. Don't worry. They'll get a man to deal with it."

Ahmed moseyed past me towards the men's residence. Apparently deadly snake sightings were nothing to worry about. And who was this hero that would deal with the lethal cobra? An Indian form of animal control or maybe a swami snake-charmer?

But then I saw 'the man'. The little old Hindu that worked as construction worker, gardener, and general servant for the university was heading my way. The same old Hindu who a few weeks back was ordered by the administration to enter my room, without my knowledge, and to move my belongings to a new residence. I had run into him on my way back from lunch, his arms piled high with my books, my makeup and my clothes complete with underwear hanging from his arm. It wasn't his decision, just his orders, so to mask my annoyance at such an invasion of privacy, I bought the old Hindu a cup of chai in thanks for his service, his gratitude embarrassing. Since then, he had smiled at me whenever we crossed paths, holding his palms together in front of his face and bowing his head. Tiny and shriveled with the horizontal markings of Shiva on his forehead, he'd moved past a westerner's retirement age decades ago.

One of the administrators yelled in the old Hindu's direction and he sped up, hurrying past me to the ditch. The driver and three men pointed into the grassy area as they barked orders at him. He didn't look at them, but he did take one hesitant step, then another, and another deeper into the thick brush. He picked up a fallen branch and continued onwards, his leathery feet disappearing from sight. He swung the stick back and forth, back and forth, I guess to scare the cobra into an appearance followed by a swift beating to death. The administrators continued to direct their commands in an increasing volume at the old man.

I stepped forward, my anxiety reaching a feverish pitch. How could this barefoot senior citizen be forced into this dreadful situation? Would I see an old man's life end so unceremoniously taking his last breath as these high-caste bastards yelled at him? I debated saying something, but what? As a foreigner *and* a woman, none of these men paid much attention to me anyway, especially now that I'd paid the university fees and my rent.

Then I surprised myself. A giggle escaped my lips; then a chuckle. I bit my tongue, laughing at a time like this was incredibly gauche. This was ludicrous. Who on god's green earth had decided this crazy social hierarchy? The little old Hindu was risking a painful death in order not to get fired? I felt a gush of hysterical laughter rise again. And to think I had just stumbled on this situation. What was happening around the next corner, in the next neighbourhood?

I walked past the men biting my lip to keep my laughter at bay. I headed towards my residence glancing over my shoulder at the old Hindu now wildly swinging the stick over his head and down into the brush. This time as I laughed tears formed in my eyes. As my mirth grew, I realized something: this development thing I was here in India to study had created a mistaken identity. I was not a judge, but a witness. And this laughter was not at the old Hindu, but instead was flamed by elation at my sudden release of control, a control that had held me hostage since I stepped foot in India two months prior.

If this were a fictional story, the cobra would have attacked the old Hindu. Man and serpent would wrestle, but the Hindu would eventually fall under the snake's deadly bite. That night at home alone, one of the administrators would see the life-long error of his ways. He would realize although he had been taught to view lower castes as expendable and born to serve in the dirtiest and most laborious ways, they too went home to their families at the end of each day. They too have habits and a history.

But the story ends less dramatically. I saw the old Hindu the next morning. I asked around and the servant had no luck scaring the cobra out of its hiding place. I suspect the snake was long gone by the time the old Hindu descended into the brush. Perhaps the serpent slithered through the field, stopping for a snack at the wells, continued on past the library, and back into the lush secretive jungle.

After the cobra incident, my remaining months in India were full of wonder and admiration. My regret lay only in that I hadn't realized sooner how fruitlessly frustrating it is to live as subjective observer rather at least trying to behave as objective participant. A burgeoning patience and humility replaced judgment and with this, I fell deeply in love with the ancient lands of India: her geography, her customs, her bartering and badgering, and her people; their songs, their rituals, their diversity. I spent time alone in the desert just a few miles from the Pakistani border and as one of the masses in the great grey impoverished cities: Ahmedabad, Delhi, Kolkata, Mumbai, Jodhpur, and Varansi. I slept in the ancient towers of Jalsimer and hiked the cool tea-growing mountainsides of Darjeeling, and I met people cut from many different fabrics on my journey. And through it all, I became another traveler from the west who took the lessons of this ancient land and became a better person for it.

Ho B52

Cecilia Unite

Born to Filipino parents in Halifax, Nova Scotia, Cecilia has been living and working overseas since 1998. For the past few years, she has been working in International Development, focusing on disadvantaged youth, public health, and education in Hanoi, Vietnam.

It's a heavy feeling like little claws scratching you, a slight gnawing teasing you behind the back of your eyes, slipping down your skull and resting in a tight knot on your shoulders. A flurry of gesticulation, expressive eyes and lips, and you are patiently watchful as you do nothing but hope you will figure it all out. You hope you will find resolution knowing deep down you will never really understand. Culture is pontificated, debated, academized, but when it envelops you none of that matters. While the last breaths of a friend are taken in front of you, it doesn't matter what cultural rituals are performed. Your only certainty is that he's gone.

Ho B52 or B52 Bomber Lake is a pond filled with green slime, an opaque film that has taken on a life of its own. It changes shades with the weather and moves in a uniform, jelly-like motion when it's disturbed by wind or by garbage or stones thrown into its weary depths. Ho B52 sits in the center of Ngoc Ha, a neighborhood – a village, within the maze of Hanoi, Vietnam. In the lake's center rests a peculiar trophy, a half-sunken, shot-down B52 bomber, waiting wearily, sliding slowly deeper into the mysterious depths of the pond.

I lived in Ngoc Ha deep within Hanoi. Rather than being surrounded and involved with the world around it, the village seemed unique, removed, floating in its own universe. Ho B52 sat in the centre of this universe. Row upon row of houses stared at it, circling it like a taunted child in a playground. But this story isn't about the infamous war or its remnants; it isn't about me or the place I lived, and it's not about the culture or the language of the world around me; it's about Linh.

Every Sunday, my housemate Clare and I sat on a thin moldy woven mat on the sweating tiles of Linh's shop with his family. Our house sat next to his, on one corner of the Ho B52. His shop was at the bottom of his house – a dwelling shaped like boxes stacked on top of each other and it looked out onto the sometimes dusty, sometimes muddy, sometimes flooded road that circled Ho B52. Linh's family wasn't particularly rich or poor, their tired looking shop had little more than candy and lottery numbers for sale, but nothing about them seemed average.

    Linh normally dressed in a thin nylon track suit and often drove me on his motorbike to work. His clothes draped loosely around his thin body flapped carelessly in the breeze as he drove off. His hair was always neatly cut and his large liquid eyes, seemingly larger than his face often looked as though he could see into another universe, into another time. His languid manner was always so calming in a place like Ngoc Ha. At times, the village suffocated you with its vitality: kids screaming, women gossiping, sellers hawking, men gambling, cocks crowing, dogs yelping. Linh's family was always needing and wanting more than what they had, but they were generally satisfied with their simple existence and this contentedness always puzzled me. I never did find out how they managed their seemingly charmed life on such a meager wage: Linh's two children even went to good schools.

    Our Sunday meal usually consisted of a hearty soup made from white fish, its cartilage-like scales hanging desperately onto its flesh. The fish was caught, no doubt, in one of the polluted ponds or rivers near the city. Anh Khanh, the fisherman and Linh's best friend, looked as though he walked straight out of a '70's disco, decked out in gold aviator sunglasses, hair dyed a bit too black, a toothy grin, and tattoos scrawled over his dark skin that told of secret stories.

    I left those meals a little red faced from the rice wine, full from the fish and noodles, cramps in my thighs and pain in my knees from sitting on the bamboo mat for hours, never understanding more than a few sentences. Sometimes I wondered if Anh Khanh, his wife, and Linh's family felt as I did; the throbbing ache of wonder about another culture, oblivious of my life as I was of theirs. My head ached and yearned for respite from all the questions I had and words I wanted to speak, but that dull ache oddly always made me feel good.

    The grey damp winter that year in Ngoc Ha was the kind that makes your bones creak and your flesh shudder, but it ended as quickly as it came. By the spring, the B52 bomber seemed a little more sunken, a little more tired.

With the sunshine and the stifling humidity came the Lunar New Year and the promise of another year more successful, prosperous, and healthy than the last. As the New Year passed, homes were filled with goods, children played with their new toys, and the last sticks of incense burned in prayer for the hopes of the new year. But Linh was not at home sitting inside the freshly painted walls of his shop; nor was he buzzing around on his motorbike. Days and weeks passed and confusion and concern grew bubbling under the surface until Linh's wife finally told Clare and I in whispers that Linh was in the hospital.

Some said cancer, others said pneumonia, and the list of potential treatments was prescribed by anyone who thought their wisdom and knowledge worth the words. But then Linh came home and there was nothing anyone could do. Everyone knew what it was, but it was too shameful to talk about openly. People whispered, sharing their knowledge, but they didn't share it with us, the people from outside of their universe.

Linh's little family shop became a makeshift hospital. Mucus pooled in Linh's lungs, flesh clung to his skin. A bamboo pole held his IV and his skeletal body lay on the bone hard platform of a bed. The moaning and sweating, the agony clung to him like a thick oozing tar. His sweat soaked hair matted to the mouldy pillow, the yellow of his eyes begged, pleaded until his wife finally gave him respite from the needle that got him there in the first place.

In the end, she smothered him. He died surrounded by the wise elders, his family, his friends, and his next door neighbours: the people from another universe. My ears and throat strained as I pushed back liquid into my eyes, silently screaming. My head spun at what was happening; at the nod of an exact time on an exact day: the precision of luck. Linh was sent to yet another universe far beyond the one we understood as our reality.

The colourful rituals, the incensed smells, the seemingly obscure and incomprehensible preparations became a part of me and our house – the one that shared the corner with Linh's family. The methodical motions, the tables and chairs placed in line, the cleaning, the cooking, and the movements of useless business buzzing in every corner of the front room. The opened front doors overlooked Ho B52; inside lay the funeral reception and the shop cum hospital next door became the funeral parlor. I was possessed with the confusion, the loss, the language, the traditions.

We waited in the front room for guests to arrive, to eat, to leave. We waited and prepared more food, sometimes strangers cooked and cleaned for us. We sat in the corner watching the conversations and waited for something, anything to happen.

People spoke about Linh's life and his children. The women slowly fanned themselves as they shook their heads at the loss for such a young family while simultaneously thanking their god it wasn't their loss, their family. We stayed up late and had fish soup with Anh Khanh and conversed politely about nothing and waited for what was next. The rice wine and warm beer was passed around to the men and, at times, the women who giggled as they took a sip. Then we went to bed. Three days – was it? The blur of waiting, opening our house to unfamiliar faces and sounds, sitting on hard plastic stools to face the Ho B52. We watched mosquitoes dance on the mirage of the solid green meadow mistaking the pond's surface for a place to play, unknowing of the dark liquid depths beneath.

Announcements were posted, wreaths of colorful flowers with ribbons announced messages of condolences. Linh's body was dressed in a suit and tie, his face distorted under cracked make-up; he looked nothing like the man in a tracksuit I once knew. That gnawing and straining became so thick it was hard to breathe. And as quickly as the preparations came, he was lifted and carried in a procession of friends emptying from our house, a sea of strangers and family around Ho B52. The shell of his former self was carried out of that universe leaving us on a stream of tears.

My first time hosting a funeral helped clear away some of that feeling that everyone gets when they are out of their depth and are struggling for breath and to hang onto something, anything that makes sense. Little claws scratching; a gnawing ever so slightly teasing you behind the back of your eyes as it slips down your skull to rest in a tight knot on your shoulders. You know what it feels like.

The clean-up after the funeral came and went. We gained a few extra tables and plastic chairs, boiled chicken, inedible snacks, and a deafening quiet. We swept the steps. And when enough time passed we opened our eyes and saw the B52 for what it meant to us: a reminder of our loss. When we were finally ready, we looked around us and saw Linh. We missed him, but we thanked him for helping us live in the universe where he was from.

Alternative Class for First Timers

Amanda Minaker

Amanda lives with her husband and wonderful daughter Harper. They have a mini-schnauzer named Elvis and an increasingly friendly cat, Pedro. She loves reading other authors and talking to her hilarious fellow Moms. Amanda grew up in Waverly, NY and there is no telling where she lives at the time of publication.

Although I would love to write about being pregnant for the first time, sadly it was not my first pregnancy. A lifetime ago it seems for me, I suffered an unsuccessful pregnancy. If you are anything like me, and I pray that you are not thus afflicted, then you will know the panic-inducing mood swings that a previously unsuccessful pregnancy (otherwise known as a miscarriage) can bring on. However, I can tell you that this was my first official labor… and it was a doozy.

I write this story with a smile on my face, not because I think I am somehow better than you non-baby-havers, but because I was once on the other side of this mysterious curtain- desperate for a little foreknowledge of exactly what I was going to inevitably face. I feel your pain.

I did many things that first-time parents do. My husband and I dutifully attended the classes suggested by our obstetrician. Here is where I will pause to take a moment of reflection. We decided to attend a non-traditional class about birthing. Let me just say, there is a reason very few (actually NONE) second time moms are in this class. Once you know the flavor of the ice cream is epidural, few women bother to look at the other flavors if you know what I mean. Don't get me wrong, I had the purest of intentions. I was set in mind and heart to go completely natural. And I did. For two and a half days. I'm not kidding. Ask my very wonderful husband and the complete rotation of nurses at my hospital. And we knew them all by the end, and boy, did they know me!

By 32 weeks, my normal pregnancy did what I had been dreading it would do… it became abnormal. I was shuttled from an appointment to the hospital for a "non-stress test" which should be known as "causes heart palpitations, crying and false labor due to the fact that you are most positively STRESSED test." I had bravely faced the appointment alone that day- the first one during the pregnancy that my dear hubby couldn't attend- and I had to call him and tell him the news. He rushed over there to see me in bed, hooked up to monitors completely unhinged. All tests came back fine. I ended up on bed rest anyway due to my blood pressure being high and there was protein (blood) in my urine. Too much information you say? Oh, just wait, my friend. It gets better.

I want to take a moment to perhaps shed some light on why my blood pressure may have been high at this point in my pregnancy. We had recently backed out of a house deal with the market being tough and impending parenthood looming. We decided we had enough on our plate. It upset my husband's family (long story), and we were on strained speaking terms- after several months of no terms to speak of at all. This situation had led us to live- "temporarily"- with my sister, her husband, two kids, their dog, us, our dog, cat and a partridge in a pear tree! Ok, no partridges really but all these beings were living- temporarily- in a two bedroom apartment. For 4 months! And my parents only lived 5 minutes away. Perhaps it was not pregnancy-induced hypertension but in fact life-induced hypertension? Gee, ya think?!?!

I was ordered on bed rest although I felt fine. Well, eight and a half months pregnant but fine. Bed rest didn't quite compute in the house and I would either be bullied into staying in bed (husband) or be chided to get it myself (refuse to name names). The doctors saw me every other day to check my blood pressure. Are you okay now? Are you okay now? What about now? Still okay? Blood pressure still high? They even checked me into the hospital- which was restful, if not weird and scary. They put me in the recovery wing- so I got to see all these women who were glowing and pushing around their tiny bundles- there I am scared shitless that I would not in fact EVER get to be in their booties.

So after a few weeks of the hypertension checking carousel, on our third (or was it our fourth?) non-stress test they decided to check me in and induce me. Luckily, I was a pro at this point and had packed an overnight bag and anything I might need for the next month for that matter. I may seem cavalier about it now, but at the time I felt totally overwhelmed, unprepared and scared witless.

I remember being ready for labor to immediately begin with the first bag of pitocin… ah how naïve I was. After a day and a half with very little progress made I was slightly more than down in the mouth- let's just say that doctor still probably thinks I hate her! I "rested" overnight- after a sleep inducing medication was given. I slept fitfully for a few hours- then woke up, ate and it was back to the "pit" I go!

At one point, late that Saturday night I finally made it to three, count 'em THREE, centimeters! Hallelujah choruses were singing as they announced I would now be administered an epidural. At this point, even if it wasn't something they told me I had to do- for blood pressure- I hate to admit I would have considered it. It wasn't so much for the pain. I had breathed through that for 48 plus hours. It was the fact that the epidural relaxed me, once the second attempt was successful, so much that I progressed SEVEN centimeters in about an hour. Not kidding. My sister left thinking it wasn't going to happen and had to rush back to make it just in time to see me push out my daughter. It was my own personal illustration of 0 to 60 (or at least in this case 0 to 10).

And now… for the best part: PUSHING!!! Maybe it was the epidural, or the kegels done dutifully all those months or the exhaustion of labor, but for me the most amazingly exhilarating hour of all was the pushing. It was honest to goodness work (and frustrating to not know why I couldn't just get her out already) but MAN was that rewarding stuff! I was so happy to be able to do some real work and know we were so close to meeting our little fighter that nothing could have been better. Except for of course, seeing her and then being her mom- which still hasn't sunk in even five months later. I think at one point, I looked up at the lovely doctor and said, "Hi. This is great." Or something to that effect. It is a bit fuzzy to be honest.

You may have been warned that women will stop you on the street once you or your partner start showing (or at least once they know you have been THERE) and will bond with you over shared stories. You may even find that you are less annoyed and more fascinated with the tale. No two stories are exactly alike in the way of snowflakes. Many women will really sell their story (written sarcastically). They practically gave birth in a field while walking to school uphill both ways in the snow. And maybe you will feel your birthing that way. But most of all, it is this experience that is not quite your nightmares and not a walk in the park exactly. Although, you may end up walking quite a bit, most people are confined to doing it in the hallways of Labor and Delivery Ward. The scenery is a little boring but you won't really notice.

     So, after my explanation by this first time mom of labor- do I have any sage advice? Yes. Take a camera with charged batteries and a hairbrush and then only take a picture of you and the baby and your partner of choice. Then put that camera to use taking all the baby pictures you can- you are going to be a bit camera shy, sister! Oh and relax… labor is only as bad as you make it. (Laughs) At least that is what we learned at our alternative birth class.

Elegy To My Marriage

Cecilia Hutchinson

Cecilia's childhood was spent in Atlantic Canada on a small island off the coast of Newfoundland. She now lives in the land-locked Canadian Prairies where she is constantly reminded of the spiritual connection between the wide, open Prairie sky and the vast Atlantic ocean. Clear days offer an unlimited view of sky or sea; overcast days share the same impediments of water in cloud, mist, and rain.

It's every girl's dream, they said, and so I dreamed of marriage,
Dreamed of living intimately with another, sharing love, laughter and life.

We soon learned the old politician was correct when he said,
"One must enter marriage with eyes wide open and live it with eyes half shut."

But what if eyes half shut cannot keep the differences at bay?
We either quit immediately -- or stay. Follow mother's dictum,
"If you make a hard bed you must sleep in it!"

Oh marriage, it was eyes half shut that enabled the birth of our children;
Eyes half shut that moved us through their youth and early adulthood;
Eyes half shut that helped stifle and quiet raw emotions,
To 'do the best we could' to keep a family for the children.

What happens to marriage when eyes half shut are startled wide open?
When catastrophe forces clarity and light?
Like the philosopher who finds truth and cannot ignore it,
Try as I might, I could no longer live with my eyes half shut.

Marriage, you ideal social institution,
We like to think you hold our system together.
Marriage, I salute you.
As a middle-aged, experienced individual with eyes wide open,
I take you off your pedestal.
And, quite clearly, I say goodbye to you,
For I no longer live with eyes half shut.

Potatoes for Ethiopia

Shirley Pashley

Born and raised in Montreal, Quebec, Shirley Pashley recently moved to Fredericton, New Brunswick. An academic at heart, Pashley spends her time trying to advocate human rights in practice rather than merely in writing... This piece is the most light-hearted work she's ever written about the issue she takes most seriously. Once world peace is established, Pashley looks forward to spending her time enjoying the wonders of nature around the world, as well as her love of animals and cupcakes.

"Eat everything on your plate, there are starving children in the world" is a common phrase to many North American children. It has certainly stayed with me throughout my life. From the first time I heard it, I wondered who these starving children were and why we weren't feeding them.

I never had much of an appetite as a child so finishing everything on my plate was always a gruelling task. Luckily, I had a father who felt the same obligation, or so I assumed, because he always finished everything on his plate *and* on mine if the need arose. I was seven years old when on yet another meatloaf and potatoes night, I couldn't help but think, "I know I'm supposed to finish everything on my plate and be grateful for everything I'm fed, but these potatoes are just so bland, I think I might gag if I have to force down one more forkful!"

The day prior, I had been watching what little television I was permitted, and I was intrigued by an hour-long special about starving children in Ethiopia. It was my first time being exposed to this issue other than my parents' well-intended guilt-trips at dinner time. These young black children lived in what appeared to be a desert; some of them lived in little shacks made from cardboard, while others just lived out in the open among piles of garbage. Some children had protruding stomachs from various diseases; others were as skinny as twigs. Some had flies all around them; others had physical ailments from disease. I was shocked. Horrified. Depressed. Angry. That is a lot of emotion for a seven year old. I couldn't shake the awful feeling that it was wrong, and that someone had to do something about it.

So that evening as I attempted to force down my meatloaf and potatoes, I thought of the perfect solution. "I'll send them to Ethiopia!" I knew my food wouldn't feed the whole country, but at least one child might not go to bed on an empty stomach that night! Isn't that all we need - to all give our leftovers to the hungry of the world? That way, we wouldn't have to stuff ourselves past the point of being full, they wouldn't have to starve, and nothing would be wasted!

I took my plate upstairs. I removed an envelope from the desk drawer where I'd watched my mother take envelopes to address Christmas cards. I dumped my potatoes inside, flipped the envelope around, and wrote "Ethiopia" on the front.

Hmm, how could I make sure it got there? Should I write a note and include it with my potatoes? Surely the people in Ethiopia would figure it out. My mum would know what to do. She could probably put a stamp on it for me and mail it too; that way, it would get there for sure.

I took it to her and asked her to mail it for me. She smiled and seemed proud; I was sure it would get there. Maybe Santa Claus could deliver it if the mailman wouldn't, even if it was summer-time. Surely, Santa would know where to find Ethiopia. My mom could probably take it to *him*.

~~~~~~~~~~~

Fourteen years later, I enrolled in a Political Science class in my third year of university. The class focused on international relations, specifically on the inequalities between 'First-world' and 'Third-world' nations, also referred to as 'developed' and 'developing' countries (the implication being that advanced technology and more money meant we Western countries were more developed). The class also studied how rich nations took advantage of poor nations. Rich nations were rich because they kept poor nations poor. Well, that may be a little simplified, but I'd soon discover people often tended to make it sound more complex to justify it.

My professor told us about the living conditions of people in 'developing' nations.

Ethiopia...

That sounded inaccurate. Who are we to say they're "developing" – is it because we think they are on their way to being completely "*developed*", like us? How obnoxious of us. Why is it all about technology, industry, money? Maybe these people had it made, had the fundamentals of life down pat, but we just wanted more money, so we took from them: their resources; their willingness to work for next to nothing; and now we think we're happier than them.

My professor told us about the awful conditions in factories where women and children made all the luxuries we buy in North America. I was stunned. *How can this be?* We know about these conditions and we still buy stuff like there's no tomorrow? Throw stuff out when we are sick of it and buy more when a new model comes out? Do these women and children at least get to take some home for themselves? *Ha!* What is wrong with this picture?!

My professor told us about the ILO – the International Labour Organization, whose main responsibility is to monitor labour conditions around the world. They are the institution who documented all the horrid facts I was hearing: no bathroom breaks; no windows; inhaling chemicals all day; rapes committed by supervisors; firings for the consequential pregnancy.

I lifted up my hand – my first time doing so since the third grade, when my teacher made fun of me for asking a "dumb question." "If the International Labour Organization knows all this stuff is going on, and if it's all illegal, how come they aren't doing anything about it? How come nobody's stopping it?"

My professor chuckled. I didn't know what that meant. Was he making fun of me, just as my third grade teacher had done? Was it a stupid question? Had he already given the answer and I wasn't paying attention? What? WHAT?

It was like my first time learning about Ethiopian children all over again. Wasn't there a simple solution to all of this? Couldn't we just stop exploiting others? Couldn't we all send our potatoes to these people and solve the problem of world hunger? Why am I the only one who thinks it's that easy? Am I still thinking like a seven year old? Is it that ridiculous? Am I that naïve? Why do things like economic systems and bureaucratic procedures get in the way of solving solvable problems? Do we have to make things so complicated? Or are we just greedy, or scared of change, or what? *WHAT? Why do humans treat each other this way? Are we chemically imbalanced as a species?*

Call me a simple-minded seven year old. I'll be flattered. Sometimes, first times happen over and over again. I hope this one never gets old. That'll be the day I've given up.

Warning! This is not a toy

Kim Jones

Kim currently lives in Madrid, Spain with her husband and son. She returns to her home of New Brunswick, Canada every summer to spend time with family and friends.

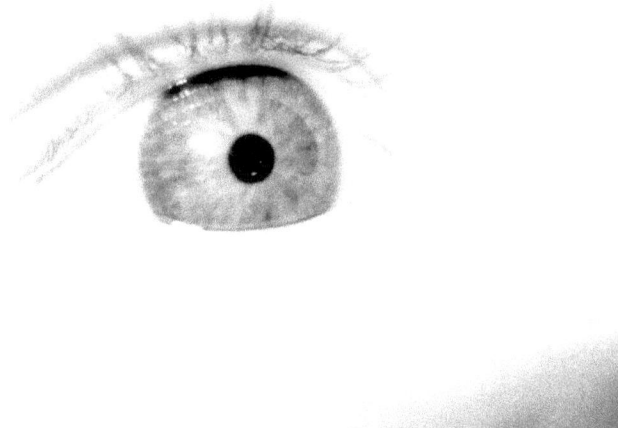

It seemed like having a baby had suddenly become fashionable. Just like acid-washed jeans in the eighties and sushi in the nineties. Everywhere I looked I saw baby-mania: actresses proudly showing off round bellies, some charging millions for photographs of their newborns. A Galician woman in her late sixties becomes the oldest woman in the world to give birth to twins. Not-so-young yummy mummies push 1000 Euro prams with one hand while busily chatting away on the newest cell phone model, their new blue or pink buddle the perfect accessory.

I couldn't tell if having a baby was suddenly in style or if it was just me noticing this baby-mania for the first time. It could be that I was thirty-one and ready to have a baby.

The fact is I always wanted a baby and by always, I mean as far back as I can remember. As a little girl I knew I physically couldn't have a baby no matter how much I desired one so instead, I begged my parents for another brother or sister. As a pre-teen I got my first chance to take care of a baby when my mother decided to look after three young boys. In my late teens I imagined what it would be like to have a baby with my boyfriend and what kind of father he would be to our child.

All this time imagining babies, I never pictured myself getting married or having a lasting and loving relationship. The thought of *forever* with the same man scared me. It seemed too decisive, unchanging, and final. No more boyfriends? No more wondering about this guy or that guy? I guess the hardest part of imagining myself in a lasting relationship was the fear of leaving behind all of the lives I could have lived as a single, or at least, unmarried woman.

As it turned out married life was not as final as I had thought. My husband Javi and I have changed and grown as separate people within our marriage. Javi is my media-naranja (my half orange) as they say here in Spain; he was waiting for me all along although I had to fly across the ocean to find him. After we met, I left for Canada only to revisit Madrid, just to leave and return again. It was this second time returning to Spain I finally knew what it meant to be a whole with someone and a half without.

It was just a few days ago, I really understood the expression media naranja. In Spain most people like to squeeze their own orange juice in the morning. I had my oranges all cut down the middle ready to squeeze and I was trying to find the other half of one as to divide it evenly into two glasses. I carefully selected two halves that appeared to be a whole, but when I put them together it was obvious they were not from the same orange. I tried another promising half, then another. I finally found the missing half and twisted the two pieces into each other to fit perfectly. That is who my life partner is, someone with whom I have become seamless. Sentences are finished, thoughts are shown in a movement or a glance. Happiness is shared.

My decision to have a baby with Javi had nothing to do with any trend. Believe it or not, it had nothing to do with my biological time clock ticking either. (Or my rice overcooking as they also say here in Spain.) It certainly wasn't about stability: we are still renting and Javi´s job isn't permanent, but I don't think there ever is a perfect time. For me, however, there were less perfect times: like living in a foreign country without work papers, or living with chronic urticaria and spending a year contracting hives from anything from laundry detergent to sliced ham. So in the end I thought if there is no perfect moment to have a baby than this one is as good as any and better that some. Thus I entered the world of ovulation charts and folic acid with my fingers crossed.

The first month of 'trying' I was certain I was pregnant. My breasts were sore, I felt bloated, I even had a few cravings.

"Five days late, I'm never five days late," I told Javi for the tenth time." Jess said her sister had a false negative test and... Are you listening, Javi?"

"Mmmm," he lied.

"What did I just say then?" I quizzed, but Javi was good at this game. He's often able to repeat words back without actually listening; it must be from years of repeating verbs in English class.

"Jess said her sister had a test," he mumbled without thinking.

"A-ha, you weren't listening!" I fired back.

I got my period the next day. It's annoying how pregnancy symptoms are the same as PMS.

Trying to get pregnant was already frustrating and I had only been trying for a month! I was edgy and annoyed. Every extra coffee I drank or heavy grocery bag I hauled home was filled with worry: what if I'm hurting a little fetus inside me? I had a new respect for women who have difficulty conceiving. The uncertainty of being pregnant is constantly running through your head like a guilty conscience.

The following month was better. I decided not to obsess so much as this might take a while. I was invited to a Christmas party at a fellow teacher's house.

"A glass of wine would be nice," I mentioned to my co-worker Jess, "or a bottle."

I was pretty sure I wasn't pregnant; I had been spotting for over a week and was just waiting for my period. I was in a horrible mood that morning on the way to work and my husband was doing everything wrong, normal PMS. But since the party was Friday night I decided to buy a pregnancy test to take Friday morning so I could drink without worry.

Friday morning I woke up and took the test while Javi and I were busy hurrying to get ready for work. Half asleep I read the instructions again: "OK one line test works, two pregnant... wait five minutes." That would give me time to wake up. Two clear and intense blue lines appeared within seconds. I blinked surprised by the speed and shocked by the results. My jaw dropped. "J...J...Javi."

"You're pregnant? I knew it." We grinned and hugged, but I don't think either one of us believed it. It was too easy. I kept reminding myself: I'm not alone anymore; someone is growing inside of me.

The morning went on as usual. I shoveled in breakfast while brushing my hair and, before I knew it I was at school. By that time my news had sunk in. I was ecstatic and wanted to share my joy with someone. Luckily I spotted Jess, someone I could confide in. I hurried her into the bathroom and looked under the stalls for feet. When I was sure we were alone I whispered with a grin from ear to ear, "Jess, I took the test and I'm pregnant!"

She squealed with delight. "I'm so happy for you."

She gave me a huge hug. Mid-hug Merce walked in. Merce is the toughest teacher in the country. Rather than the typical pre-school teacher, Merce looks more like a bike gang leader with her short leather jacket, stompy walk, straight face, and masculine voice that utters grunts rather than words.

She mumbled some sort of greeting at us and we quickly broke our hug. If there is one thing I've learned about St. Stephen's School, it's that gossip is passed on quickly. People know you're engaged before you do. This was such personal news I didn't want anyone else to know just yet. The one thing that would make a miscarriage worse was to have eighty teachers know about it.

But hey Merce was a Spanish teacher; as far as I knew her English was basically non-existent. I wasn't worried until Jess found me in the cafeteria to warn me that Merce had spread a rumor that either Jess or I was pregnant. Why else would we hug? I was furious! How dare she make rumors out of her assumptions! How could someone wreck my day of bliss?

The worst part was I was angry at Jess. Why didn't she deny I was pregnant more convincingly? Why did she give me that damn hug in the first place? She should have known better, been more discreet.

I decided to be pro-active and start a new rumor about myself explaining the hug; maybe I could erase the damage. I found Mel, the English teacher who spreads gossip like the wind and lied about Javi getting a raise and how happy we were. It didn't fly, not juicy enough. Whispers of my possible pregnancy went on behind my back, but no one ever asked me. When I finally announced my pregnancy at work most people already knew, but the teachers I really cared about put on a surprised smile and hugged me all the same.

That Friday evening, I began to bleed. I called to make a doctor's appointment, but the receptionist told me there were no openings until next month. She instructed me to go to the Emergency Room. Teary eyed I called Javi at work and we went to the hospital for our first ultrasound. The doctor told me I was getting a 'baja medica' and to rest for two weeks. The doctor also said I could forget about my trip home to Canada for Christmas.

A 'baja medica' is something most Spanish people think they want. It is a paper signed by a doctor that allows you to stay home, rest, and recuperate while still receiving your regular salary. Each week you return to the doctor and your baja medica is either renewed or not. Co-workers complain about people getting 'bajas' for something minor and often boast of being offered one and refusing it.

I looked at my 'baja' paper and under reason it clearly read 'Risk of Miscarriage.' I took it very seriously; I sat on my couch not moving, willing my little fetus to stay put and grow. My spotting stopped immediately and, after a week I was free to move. The day before my flight left for Canada I was granted permission to travel.

I spent Christmas with my family, throwing up my breakfast, and sitting on the recliner. I barely remember being there.

In January I was back in Madrid and my appetite went into overdrive. The smell of coffee, cigarettes, and wine all disgusted me. I put all my energy into the pregnancy, buying magazines, and following the fetus growth charts. Whenever someone would enter the teacher's room and say something like; "Oh, what a nice day," or "Look at this story in the newspaper," I would just smile and try to steer the conversation towards my pregnancy. If someone would indulge me, I could talk about my unborn baby, what I was going to buy, possible names, and more until they fell asleep or found an excuse to leave.

At four months, I began to bleed again. We rushed to the Emergency Room. At nine o'clock on a Sunday morning the place was practically empty except for another couple. I sat down beside Javi and balled my eyes out for the three minutes it took for the nurse to call my name.

The ultrasound showed that the baby was well but they gave me a 'baja' just in case and instructed me not to move too much. The rest of my pregnancy was a mixture of working and time off. My baby seemed okay, but no one was sure what was causing the bleeding. I was overly cautious and quite bored the remainder of my pregnancy and began to wonder if this pregnancy was ever going to end. It felt like I had been waiting for years for the baby to arrive. When would I see my feet again?

Then early one morning my water broke.

I won't go into the gory details of my labour. Everyone has heard the horror stories. I was never afraid of the actual labour; I figured what is a day of pain when later I'll have a lifetime with my son, but by the seventh hour of contractions that came every three minutes, I thought differently.

I realized three things that day: I understood why a woman would want to have an abortion if she didn't want the baby; I didn't understand how someone could give up a baby for adoption after so much pain even with all the papers signed. Rip the damn papers!; and thirdly, I would never understand how someone could have a second child! After Joseph was born, I told everyone, "Yes, I know he's perfect but I'm never having another one". Luckily for brothers and sisters, pain cannot be remembered. Now, eight months later, I would love to have even more than the two children I had originally planned for.

I knew the facts. Spain had more caesarean births than any other European country, but for some reason it just never entered my mind that I would have one. What? With these birthing hips? No problem.

So I literally started to shake with fear when the doctor decided it would be a caesarean birth. My legs trembled and my arms twitched as I protested as they rolled me into the operating room. "No, no, no. Why am I having a caesarean?"

I blamed it on the midwives. One of them had arrived at an earlier stage of my labor, grabbed my stomach with both hands, and shook with all her might. I wanted to scream, but I just threw her hands off me and asked, "What are you doing?"

"Oh, just trying to wake him up" she smirked, turning on her witch heels and flying away.

Speaking Spanish while incredibly nervous and in pain was not fun. My accent grew thicker. I felt foreign; everyone and everything seemed very alien to me. In a hospital full of enemies, my constant, my deep breath, my husband was now being taken from me as they rolled me into the operating room. My instinct was to run home and have my baby under the bed or in the closet like a cat. "Don't touch me! Leave me alone!" I wanted to scream at these strangers.

Finally I was drugged and strapped down. My glasses were taken off so I couldn't see anything, not that I had much to look at except a curtain covering me at chest level. Better this way I thought. Seconds went by like minutes, all my hopes and fears waiting, waiting, waiting. And then, nineteen hours after my water broke, Joey was born and I heard the most beautiful sound, my baby crying as they hurried him away. I knew then that a mother could never misplace her baby; the cry alone is instantly etched in your brain.

The anesthesiologist gave me my glasses and the midwives showed me my baby as best they could. I wanted to hold him, but my arms were strapped down. I couldn't peel my eyes off him, but I could hardly see him either. "We are going to show him to Papa," said one of the midwives.

You can't show him little Joey. I'm supposed to do that, or at least be there. But I was being stitched up and they were already gone.

We went home a few days later. I can't remember when it happened, the exact moment escapes me or maybe it was too gradual to pinpoint, but the fantasy of having a baby and the reality of taking care of my son wasn't instant. At first I looked at little Joey thinking, "Where did you come from?" but at some point that changed to "Of course it was you in there all this time. How could I not have known before?"

A sense of completeness, of true love, the world making sense, an inner peace, a timelessness all from a little baby boy. I was overwhelmed by a notion that he had chosen us to be his parents and we choose him to be our child. He was more spirit than body at birth. I think that is what makes the experience somewhat inexplicable; something you have to do to fully understand. Even now, as I look at Joseph, light bursts through his eyes, and I know my only goal as his mother is to keep that spirit bright.

The Chalice

Nathan Cutler

Nathan obtained his Bachelor Of Arts in Education and Master degree in Educational Psychology from Memorial University of Newfoundland and a Certificate of Theology at Saint John's Theological College in Nottingham, England. He currently works as a counselor/therapist with at-risk youth.

The Californian sun bathed us in its warm rays as we strolled around the winery on our first Sunday in Napa Valley. The blue sky, the scent of vineyards about to spring into new life, the green rolling countryside was heavenly. And most delightful of all I was accompanied by my eldest child and her four month old daughter.

"Have you thought about a short story yet?" asked my daughter as she placed our newest family member into my cup-shaped arms. The flow of this new wine from her arms to mine was undertaken with the gentle ease that only mothers do naturally: the slow, caring, yet firm hold of confidence, trust, and joy.

This new mom was giving me her precious bundle so she could walk with her own mother into the crowded winery's tasting room. As this bundle of joy now rested in my arms a sudden rush of excitement, pride, and joy rushed through my whole body. Turning to go she asked again, "So have you thought about a story for my project?"

I didn't answer; my emotional elevation transporting me suddenly back to a Sunday morning many years ago. A morning when I experienced for the first time an intoxicating pleasure brought on by the contents of a very different cup: a chalice. My whole being seemed to travel to another time: back to that Sunday morning in my home-town, to the far-east regions of the western hemisphere. The content of the chalice was not so unlike the bundle cupped in my arms this morning: a source of euphoria.

In my mind's eye, I saw my mother in the kitchen before church. "Don't forget to bring home your cassock and surplice," she said as I closed the door and headed towards the Anglican Church. She had reminded me every so often to bring home the two garments I now wore each Sunday for cleaning and pressing. The church like most in that time and place was a thriving community of the faithful.

I had been an altar boy for a year now, a year since confirmation, a year since my first communion, and a year of Sundays as crucifer and server. The move from sitting in the family pew to the sacred place of the high altar to assist the Priest in the weekly Eucharist was salvation; a rescue from the stern glances of older congregational members especially when my twin brother and I took to tormenting each other in the silence of the huge nave as we waited for the church service to begin.

Becoming an altar-boy also placed me out of harm's way of the ancient looking sidemen, any of whom would click me and my brother on the back of our heads if it looked as though we threatened to shatter the stillness of this holy place during the droning sermon. The sermon surely must have been the only time in the week when each second had sixty minutes. For me to sit still for such a long time was impossible and thus led to reprimands from my older sister or one or another of my parents once we left the church and arrived home.

The reward of assisting the priest was now as altar boy I was kept busy, from the opening processional to the priest's final dismal and the recessional. There would be no idle time in between. Besides, it seemed so much like being in a Christmas concert each week. The lighting of the candles, carrying the crucifix, assisting with all the holy hardware, cleaning the large gold chalice (that seemingly mystical drinking vessel), and preparation and clearing of items from the sanctuary as the congregation filed from the church after the service into a new week.

For a moment I was back to the church where a delectable and utterly transcending experience was reoccurring, right in the church sacristy: the small room that held the holy vessels, wine, wafers and special vestments of priests and altar boys. The sacristy was the inner room which was not open to anyone else with the exception of those carrying a special message or a delivery, a place in which one only spoke in near whispers as preparations were made for the service. It was as special to me, a fourteen year old boy, as I imagined it was for the priest and the others that assisted him.

The following Wednesday the voice of my stern God-like math teacher Mr. Hatcher's jerked me forward in my seat. "What are you smiling about? Attend to your work."

Little could he know my smile was one of relief and acceptance of what happened that previous Sunday morning and that here I sat accepting, without guilt, without remorse, or any sense of sin or sorrow something that was a first-time for me. I now knew what it was like to be intoxicated.

I was the last one in the church after Sunday's service. I had cleaned the holy vessels and placed them in their respective slots in the cupboard placing the wine bottles in the wine rack on the bottom shelf. I checked that all candles were properly extinguished and that the sacristy was now in order with all vestments properly stowed away, my own clothing hung on the door latch so I wouldn't forget them.

As the door to the sacristy closed behind me, I saw it on the side table: a bottle of wine. I had failed to stow it away with the others. I didn't really even think about my next action as I stood in the midst of the lingering smell of recently extinguished candles and the after-taste of one small sip of rich red wine.

With neither rhyme nor reason I reached for the large gold chalice, cupping it with a care and gentleness, as if it were an infant, and with my other hand popped the cork of the unfinished and half full bottled wine. The wine flowed from the bottle into the golden chalice with the sweetest of aromas, the twinkling of the heaven's stars, and the gentle settling of a child into a mother's arms. I filled the shiny, transfixing vessel to the very top and elevated the Chalice to my lips kissing the surface ever so softly and then with the uncouth dignity of a late night drunk slurped and gulped the remains of the bottle.

With each gulp I rotated the chalice making quarter turns clockwise as I had observed the priest doing during the end of the Eucharist. One move for each direction of the compass or so I thought. "Where did I ever get that notion?" I wondered aloud.

By the fourth quarter the slurping and gulping had stopped. Gently I re-cleaned the chalice as if bathing a newborn child, re-corked the now-empty bottle, and hid it in the far reaches of the wine cabinet.

I hurried through the church. As the door securely shut behind me and the fresh breeze rushed into my lungs, I was suddenly engulfed by a tingling and quivering of my whole body. Numbness clothed me as if I was getting sleepy and I became ever aware of my every sense, aware of myself from head to toe. Without a care in the world I found my two feet bouncing me along the road heading home…home… With each step the elation coupled with the numbness seemed odd and giddy but odder still I heard myself as if with an angelic voice singing some chorus from Sunday school …Jesus loves me this I know.

All I could think of now was the warm feeling, the light-headiness, how good I felt, and the heightened sense of everything around me. Yes, it certainly felt good. The feeling inside of me was one I savored even more than the roast chicken and all the trimmings waiting for me on the kitchen table around which my parents and five brothers and sisters patiently waited for my arrival.

Underlying my giddiness was an anxiety the family would know that my being fifteen minutes late was a sure sign that something was amiss. If asked why I was late I would give the excuse I had to return to the sacristy for the cassock and surplice that mom had reminded me to bring home. They would see the garments gently flapping as they hung over my arm; the still clean and white crisp surplice and the deep purple cassock with its thirty-odd buttons. I had often mused if each button really stood for the thirty odd Canons of the Church as found in the prayer book or was it just a smart-ass retort when I wondered out loud to the Priest why there were so many buttons to fasten. They took forever to button from top to bottom and a real nuisance to unfasten when in a hurry to get home.

Maybe I would give myself away by the look in my eyes or maybe the desire to laugh out loud or maybe just maybe I'd let something slip. Or perhaps Mom will catch me in a lie when she asked what had kept me as they waited for me before starting dinner.

Then, as if transported, I was in the kitchen standing in front of Mom. "Good you didn't forget your cassock. Dinner is almost ready so go wash your hands."

In the bathroom, I stood in front of the mirror and I saw me: full of joy, a twinkle in the eye, smiling and still humming a familiar tune, and all the while convincing myself that it's okay. I was sure God would only muse rather than punish; he would leave that to my parents if they ever found out.

Over all the years between then and now, nothing has given me such a wonderful feeling, not even the wines of Napa Valley. I had my first moment of intoxication by way of an ancient golden chalice all those years ago and now forty-four years later that elation was finally equaled by the soft breathing life cupped ever so gently in the chalice shape of my arms on this beautiful Californian Sunday.

The memory broke as my eldest returned to my side gazing down at the peaceful bundle of her child resting with her granddad. Her four-month old gift basked in the brilliant glow of new life radiating contentment from where she drifted in the realm of sleep. She was a different sacredness.

"Let's go find Grammy on the balcony over the wine tasting rooms."

I rocked and swayed my grand-daughter drinking in deeply from the chalice, a treasure nestled across my chest. I was transfixed by a pair of beautiful blue eyes as they opened wide and held mine; as though ordained she gazed at me as I hummed some old familiar tune.

She held my watery eyes captive for one brief moment as if to say: Hey Granddad what ya thinking? What mischief have you been up to? I gently closed the old memory gate and leaned down to kiss her, drinking in this most precious gift of the gods.

Small Town Girl

Michelle Osmond

Michelle Osmond recently returned to Canada after residing in Frankfurt, Germany for three years. While in Frankfurt, she spent much of her time home-schooling her two children which allowed her to introduce them to many European destinations including Pisa and Pompeii. While in Frankfurt, Michelle also honed her adoration of rich European chocolate.

I am a small town girl. My heart belongs to a remote fishing community on the coast of Labrador, Canada - population 250. My family moved around a bit when I was growing up, but we always managed to make our way back to Labrador's beautiful rugged coastline. I moved away from my family when I was eighteen years old to finish my university degree. After meeting the love of my life in 1990, and then spending the next few years moving across Canada as a military family, it would still be nine more years before I ventured across the Atlantic Ocean for my first trip to Europe.

In February of 1999, my husband was sent to Bosnia on a military tour. He was scheduled to be gone for six months, and as is customary during this type of military peacekeeping tour, he was given three weeks vacation leave. We didn't have any children at the time, so he chose to take his leave more towards the beginning of the tour, as soldiers with families tended to prefer their vacation leave in the middle of a tour. He called and told me that his vacation leave was going to be 04-21 March. I was excited to see him again.

I then had one of my brilliant ideas. Instead of him coming home to Canada for his leave, I decided to meet up with him in Europe so we could go backpacking together for three weeks. This decision, like all my great decisions, was made at the last moment. I frantically obtained a passport and international driver's license, booked a flight to Germany, and scrambled with last minute shopping items. Within three days I was on an international flight from Fredericton, Canada to Frankfurt, Germany.

I arrived in Frankfurt and after spending seven long hours on an airplane, I was greeted by security guards with guns and dogs and questions that made me stutter at the Customs counter. Why was I visiting? How long would I be staying? Where was I from? Did I have relatives in Germany? Talk about culture shock! Somehow I managed to answer all questions without hyperventilating; I successfully collected my luggage and thankfully my husband was waiting for me at our meeting point.

We spent the first couple of days in Frankfurt visiting the sights, namely a small village called Seligenstadt just twenty minutes outside the city. All of the houses looked so similar to me – like giant gingerbread houses! We also spent those first few days preparing for our three week backpacking adventure. We bought a five night Eurorail Pass which allowed us to travel on the trains throughout Europe and took care of five night's accommodations. I was so excited – I had never been on a train before. Our plan was to leave Frankfurt and then travel to Paris, France; Tarragona, Spain; Venice, Italy; Zürich, Switzerland and then back to Frankfurt. I had my *Europe on a Shoestring* book…I was ready for anything.

As this was my first time ever on a train, our friend dropped us off at the Frankfurt train station an hour early so I could check it out. I wasn't expecting the train station to be so open. Pigeons flew in and around the station, and you had to watch for their droppings! Not unlike walking on the beach in Labrador and keeping a watch out for seagull droppings. We found our train and had lots of time to find good seats. As the train started, the conductor came around and stamped our tickets. He told us that we were on the wrong car for Paris. Right train, wrong car.

"Great. The train is full now and we'll probably never find another seat." We went from car to car, looking for two empty seats. We discovered the connecting doors were hard to open. At one point we couldn't get the doors open and it took us several minutes to realize that they were still locked. We had to find a conductor to open them with his keys. The second time this happened, I was yanking with all my might on the doors when Keith yelled, "Michelle!! Stop!!" When we looked out the door into the darkness, we saw that we were at the end of the train!

Our accommodations in Paris, France were my first introduction to the "miniscule hotel rooms of Europe". The bathroom in our room was so small my six foot four husband could not shut the bathroom door while sitting in there. He had to decide what he was going to do before he went in as there was no way for him to turn around once he was situated. As well, it took a bit of time for me to get used to leaving my room key at the front desk when going out of the hotel. I realized that this was the reason that every room had its own safe. But Paris more than made up for any concerns I might have had about the hotel. We took in the spectacular sights of Paris: the Louvre's Leonardo di Vinci's Mona Lisa, Notre Dame Cathedral and it's statue of Sainte Jeanne D'Arc, Eiffel Tower (we were there Day # 298 before the year 2000), Champs-Élysées, Arc de Triomphe and its lack of road lines, the Seine River (it was really brown and smelly), and Place de la Concorde; all of the attractions that I had only ever read about in books. But my favourite part was sitting outside a Paris café having a chocolate croissant and a cappuccino watching the local people go about their business. The people of Paris, especially the women, walked with a confidence and grace I'd never noticed anywhere else in the world. I fell in love with Paris in two short days.

What I didn't fall in love with was the lack of available amenities. On our final day in Paris, we found a Laundromat. Maybe it was the constant swishing of the water (or the cappuccinos), but I really had to use the bathroom. There was no bathroom in the laundromat of course, so I had to leave my husband with the washing and go in search of a toilet. Well, as I was to discover in most of Europe, toilets are hard to find, and a clean toilet even harder to find. First, I went into a smoky bar where the "toilet" was literally a small hole in the floor; I WAS in the female washroom! There was no way I was even attempting to aim in a hole the size of a quarter. I quickly left there and went back to the café where I had had such a relaxing time earlier. There, in the back, was a nice clean toilet. I even asked if I could use it before I went it, just to make sure. No sooner was I in there and locking the door, that another customer started knocking on the door to come in as well! She knocked on the door so quickly after I went in she had to have seen me! Fortunately, it was time to continue our journey and after two days in Paris, we were back on the train on our way to Tarragona, Spain.

Tarragona is a small town on the Mediterranean coast about one hour south of Barcelona. Founded in 218 BC, it is an interesting city with an amphitheatre and Roman forum, water fountains at every street corner with potable water (not that I had any intention of drinking it. I knew my Labrador water came from a glacier – where did the Spanish water come from?), and my first sight of lemon trees growing in everyone's front yard. This was also where we were introduced to a new kind of pizza. Trying to keep food costs low, we were strolling along (okay, more like we were starving and frantically looking for something to eat) and spotted a store/restaurant selling pizzas and sandwiches. The locals were eating the pizza so we picked out a couple of slices, bought a few bottles of Coke and made our way to the beach to have a small picnic lunch. We were famished! We dug into the pizza like people possessed…only to discover that our wonderful looking pizza had fish on it! "A local specialty" as we were to find out later – it was horrible! I come from a fishing community and I love fish…but on my pizza? NEVER!

Tarragona continued to present food issues for us as we had difficulty finding somewhere to eat our evening meal. Most restaurants didn't even open until 9 pm! Not good for a couple of Canadian East Coasters who ate supper promptly at 5 pm every evening. We ended up having a "snack" at 5 pm (which wasn't so bad seeing as how we discovered we could order a beer with our Big Mac), walked around for a bit and then ate at 9 pm – as soon as the restaurant doors opened. One evening we were looking for familiar food and decided on Chinese. The restaurant was across the street from our hotel and we had made reservations the night before (after figuring out the late supper dilemma). We were surprised to see another couple in the restaurant when we showed up at 9:02 pm. After sitting down we realized that they were British. We chatted with them for a bit. We found our situation quite hilarious – we were English Canadians, sitting and chatting with a British couple, eating Chinese food in Spain!!

After five relaxing, albeit hungry, days on the Mediterranean, we headed for Venice, Italy. Venice is notable for its lack of vehicles. It is made up of 117 islands that are connected by some 150 canals and 400 bridges. As one strolls through the city, you are walking over the stones that are shifting due to the water running underneath them. This is the part in my story where I'll mention the fact that alcohol is cheaper than soft drinks and water in European countries. I took advantage of that, regardless that it takes about one beer or one glass of wine for me to be very happy.

Our first night in Venice we went out for supper (no food issues in Venice fortunately. I needed the food to absorb some of the alcohol). I got quite drunk that night in Venice and ended up eating a full Viennetta ice-cream cake. To this day I am unable to eat a piece of this ice cream dessert! The next morning we spent the day exploring the Piazza di San Marco (St. Mark's Square) and hoping the pigeons wouldn't 'drop' on us. There must have been a thousand pigeons in that square. We visited the Palazzo Ducale and the Bridge of Sighs (a thoroughfare for prisoners being led to the dungeons) where we learned that a prisoner would spend forever, guilty or not and possibly starve to death if they didn't have a family member to bring food. For a small crime such as stealing a loaf of bread, a hand would be cut off. Or maybe they would lose an ear and have it tacked to the building as a reminder to those walking by. Sure glad some things have changed in Venice.

In Zürich, Switzerland on 18 March 1999 I'm sure I swallowed a bug. We had found a nice hotel and were sleeping comfortably when I woke up and found it very difficult to swallow. I drank some bottled water and felt a tickle in my throat. Yuck. Maybe the feeling was so familiar as I have swallowed mosquitoes and sand flies before; hard not to swallow a few flies in the summertime in Labrador. Fortunately the chocolate supply in Zürich is overwhelming; I got over the "bug" incident with a bit of Toblerone and yes, more alcohol. We only spent one day wandering around Zürich, but we were fortunate to see the largest clock face in Europe (8.7 metres in diameter) at the 13th century tower of St. Peter's Church.

And then back to Frankfurt. On our second stay in Frankfurt we experienced a local flea market; tasting sausages, crepes, and mulled red wine. The architecture and history of Frankfurt are quite old, and I was able to wander through downtown and see a postcard of what the area looked like after the excessive bombing during World War II demolished the buildings. I am familiar with the circumstances surrounding the Second World War as many Newfoundlanders bravely fought in it. But to see the actual destruction was very emotional for me. I was able to see how the Germans have reconstructed the buildings and preserved the history in Römer Square. Following our wandering through the downtown area we stopped to have a glass of Äpfelwein (apple wine) in the basement of a locally owned restaurant.

It was here in Frankfurt that I bid farewell to my husband; he went back to Bosnia to finish his tour and I headed back to Canada, a beginner traveler, instilled with a new wanderlust.

The Road Less Traveled By

Patty Thille

Patty Thille is unsure about how to label herself: feminist, gardener, activist, researcher, sexual health guru wannabe, postmodern discourse nerd, health care professional? Committed to fairness, compassion, disrupting the status quo, questioning sacred cows, planting seeds for the revolution?, she finds strength in the words of EE Hale: "I am only one, but I am still one; I cannot do everything, but still I can do something; and because I cannot do everything I will not refuse to do the something that I can do."

In the late '80s, as a grade eight student, I decided to write an essay about pay equity for my social studies class. I know, quite the topic for a thirteen year old. I tripped across the concept in a Macleans magazine in my school library. To this day, I remember my astonishment at the realization that women were not paid as men were for equivalent work. Learning of this inequity disrupted the story I had been told, that people who work hard are rewarded, a story informed by my Catholic, rural Saskatchewan upbringing.

My pre-existing (and naïve) narrative was further challenged by the teacher's response to the essay. While I was given a good grade, my teacher, an older white man with decades of teaching experience, had written a counter-argument against pay equity in every inch of white space on the foolscap. This sudden jarring disconnect, the consciousness that someone in my immediate circle thought that inequality was justifiable based on sex, brought me to my first association with what is now my ideological home: feminism.

For me, feminism offered a narrative thread that could explain my previously noticed but unnamed experiences of inequity. In my limited little world, it provided a worldview by which I could understand my household and school experiences. Even at the age of thirteen, so much more in my world made sense: my father's use of anger to silence my mother's quiet strength; my parents' refusal to fight for me to be allowed to play hockey (when I tried to enroll, I was told girls were only allowed to play ringette, even if I could out-skate most of the boys my age); my physical education teacher's practice of giving the boys more floor hockey playing time than the girls; the town's habit of scheduling the girls' softball games for the potholed field, while the boys got to play on the pristinely maintained diamond; and last, but not least, the occasion I recall to this day when my grade eight teacher mocked my intelligence. The same teacher who had argued against pay equity called me '78' for a day – my mark on a math test, on display for all the class to know. The girl who was a math whiz had 'failed', and all the boys with whom I competed with for top grades knew it. My obliviousness destroyed, feminism suggested that equity was a worthy goal; one that would require much work in light of the pervasiveness of sexism in everyday life.

My mother, my rock, my only sense of the notion of 'home' was the only woman with whom I could talk with about these kinds of issues. She was a gentle, giving, compassionate and non-judgmental nurse whose emotional insight was well respected by her friends, extended family, patients, and colleagues. Part of her strength to endure my father's wrath came from the church, though she understood it as her cross to bear, something she had to endure to keep our family unit intact. My mother never encouraged me to suppress my outrage at the gender-based injustices of the world in the name of being a good woman. She tried to nurture my strong sense of justice and fairness, but she never joined me as identifying herself as a feminist.

Throughout my teens, I still had much to learn about the spectrum of feminisms, and my small Saskatchewan community, pre-internet era, had few resources to help me find my way. Enter my next first: my first Women and Gender Studies course, six years after embracing the label of 'feminist'. Only offered as a 'minor' at that time, Women's Studies exposed me to a world of critical thought and a community of activists and academics, each working in their own way to realize a vision of the future that still inspires me. Each class, I would be in awe of my fellow (mostly older) students and the professors. I would burst with energy revisiting the evening's intellectual acrobatics with my then-boyfriend on my way home every week. This introduction to Women and Gender Studies, and subsequent conversations with older women I admired pushed me to confront a new disconnect, this time an internal one: my feminist, equity-driven vision for our world, and a thread of being 'pro-life' (read anti-choice), a remnant of my Catholic upbringing.

So my nineteen-year-old self, a great admirer of my mother's way in the world, had to confront the conflict. The new women-centered vision I was offered understood termination of pregnancy as a centuries-old practice that required accessibility and safety in order to protect women's health. This vision viewed women as something more than incubators who were to be respected for knowing what is best in light of the complexities of their individual lives. My ability to actually engage in a dialogue with pro-choice peers and mentors opened up a vision that placed great value on women's lives, with all their messiness and diversity. This contrasted the dominant Catholic story I had relied upon to make sense of abortion in the past – that all human life is precious, that the context of women's lives is irrelevant to this issue. During this time, other women – academics, older coworkers, my boyfriend's feminist Catholic mother – were the first women to so palpably influence the way I thought about moral issues. My mother had not been replaced entirely; rather, I was learning to listen to more voices and decide for myself.

Over the years, this vision also created an intellectual space to understand the misuse and abuse of some and subordination of the majority to protect the greedy and the self-centered interests of a few. These feminist firsts brought to light how I could be unintentionally complicit in maintaining a system that privileges a few at the expense of many.

My subsequent years taking Women/Gender Studies courses, volunteering in women's centers, working in a feminist sex-positive store, and meeting women from a broader range of backgrounds produced wave after wave of revelations, each uncomfortable in their confrontation of what I had previously taken for granted. A brilliant essay by Peggy McIntosh called *White Privilege: Unpacking the Invisible Knapsack* led me to question my own racial privilege, and while it is a continual process to unearth the racist ideologies I learned in childhood, I am a better person for it. A peer volunteer at the university women's centre helped me understand her experiences of heterosexism. Working in a sex-positive store, a space that interrupts the story that there is such a thing as 'normal' sexuality, has created opportunity after opportunity to learn how to assume less about the people in my life. These experiences have culminated in a humbled state where I can comprehend that one could experience both discrimination and privilege. This has strengthened my determination to use my privilege for the benefit of those who are often not given a space to speak.

Not to say that this has been an easy road; each of these feminist firsts demanded I examine not only my perspectives but my behaviors. My ability to embody masculine behavior traits (competitive speech patterns such as interrupting others, or outspoken confidence even when I knew little about an issue) are likely a function of hailing from such a male dominated family where one had to cut others down to be on top. These traits had helped me be successful in my career, but I could see the destructiveness of these behaviors, how they shut down dialogue, silencing many, fostering a world that rewards arrogance and dominance over cooperation and fairness. I made the choice to confront my own 'masculine' tendencies of competitiveness that infiltrated how I interacted with others. More accurately I continue to choose to confront these dominating speech tendencies that are rewarded career wise, but perpetuate a model that I hope to disrupt. I have also had to accept that my successes are more than just an embodiment of 'good things come to those who work hard'; success is a combination of luck, privilege and only sometimes, determined hard work. I had to come to terms with how to use my privilege to help make this world a better place for everyone, not just those who shout the loudest and think they know better than others.

I did not just happen to be in the right place at the right time, meeting the right people. I was willing to listen, to re-consider everything I thought to be true or important, and I believe that it is this openness to hearing alternative views that was the critical element to my transformation into a more socially minded, and less self-centered, judgmental individual. In our egocentric, materialistic, greedy society that is North America, it would have been easier and to a degree, socially acceptable to just withdraw, remove myself from situations that illuminated such painful realities about myself and the society that we each are socialized into, and reproduce by our own actions. I see people do it around me all the time, and I can understand it is a more comfortable way to inhabit the world. Most times, I feel I chose the road less traveled by, but in my case, I know I now live in ways more consistent with my values.

Since that time, I have been able to share my feminist 'firsts' with others. In a Physical Therapy professional issues course, I chose to deviate from the suggested essay topics to write about structures of heterosexism in health care. The professor noted she had not even heard of the concept of heterosexism prior to my essay, but now recognized its importance in such a course. When working as a team coordinator in a health care setting, I was able to disrupt dominant social stories that maintain the status quo of racial and class-based privilege. Activities such as 'patient education' are geared to shaping patients into doing what we believe is best allowing them to fulfill or resume activities that support a certain economic order, rather than focusing on the development of a common understanding with patients about how best to manage their problems in their individual, complicated realities. On occasion, I have several opportunities to bridge critical, feminist social thought to mainstream health care audiences, such as talking about how fat phobia influences care, or to give workshops that model how to speak non-judgmentally with patients about sexuality. And in each of these opportunities where I create a space for reflection on how assumptions and privilege jeopardize our ability to provide patient-centered health care, I hope to plant a seed, one that can grow into a 'first' for another person.

I recognize that my 'first' presents interesting ironies. By embracing the 'label' of feminist, I have learned to suspend my reliance on the stereotypes our society uses to denigrate those different from the dominant white, heterosexual, Christian, able-bodied, middle/upper class privileged "norm". Paradoxically, I think I behave in ways more consistent with Christianity than I did in the past when I was a know-it-all Catholic. Feminism offers me strength, a sense of belonging and purpose, one of hope for a more peaceful and equitable world.

I cannot foresee what other 'firsts' are to come. Considering what I have gained through my series of feminist roads less traveled, I welcome the challenge ahead.

Sometimes You Just Have To Jump In

Anna Noble

Anna considers herself a strong and open-minded woman. Since moving to a smaller city she has begun to enjoy the simpler things of life such as long walks and painting the beautiful scenes she sees all around her.

I would not consider myself to have lived a conventional life thus far. Undertaking seemingly taboo adventures isn't so abnormal in my perspective. While some activities may seem wrong or risky at first, once you have lived through them there are often interesting stories and memories that remain. As each of these adventures must have a 'first time' they are perfect for inclusion in a chapbook about *firsts*. When thinking about first times our minds tend to wander to intimate encounters. I am no exception to this. What follows is a story about my first intimate encounter with a girl.

I met him in a gay bar, but since my best friend is gay, I considered it to be a safe and accepting environment. I later learned that he had been watching me at school and had patiently awaited a chance to meet me. I fell for him rapidly, and we were inseparable from our first night together. I quickly realized that I had met my soul mate, someone that I expected to spend many years with and with whom I would share many experiences. I was right.

By the end of our first year together he had started hinting about his desire to bring another person into our relationship. I was only twenty years old at the time and the thought of having someone else share our intimacy made me nervous so I was resistant to the idea; however, I loved him very much and I trusted him. Bisexuality was part of his personality and he was very clear about that. I had accepted the entire package when I entered into a relationship with him, so despite some initial resistance, I slowly warmed to the idea of having more than just the two of us in our relationship.

In hindsight he slowly eased me into the idea of have affairs outside of our relationship. Initially he met up with another girl and then I met up with a guy. Of course it felt like cheating, but it was also exciting at the same time. It certainly caused some friction as the jealousy was not an easy thing for me to deal with. I didn't want to share the love of my life with anyone else, yet it was so crucial to him and really it was a part of his identity. Our first experiences together with a third person were very positive and enjoyable. The fact that it was another guy at first made it very easy for me. I was the center of attention and we both were very comfortable with him. The first experience sharing our love with someone else left no bad feelings, only good ones, and opened the door to future experiences.

After a couple of years of living in a smaller city we were ready to move on to bigger and better things. Moving to a new city meant many new experiences and new encounters. Our circle of friends grew and meeting new people led to new opportunities. It also led to our first female 'third'.

Ten years later I am still in regular contact with her. She is still a skinny girl with a big smile and devilish eyes. She was a friend of a friend that we met at a party. I think she was having boyfriend troubles at the time because she seemed to latch onto my boyfriend quite quickly. In the blur of the party I didn't realize what was going on; the party was a big success and my boyfriend and I had fun both together and apart. I traveled around the party talking, dancing, and having a blast. When we left the party he had her number in his pocket and I was in a blissful daze. Over the next few days they talked on the phone and she often came to hang out with us at our apartment. So when he first told me his intentions to bring her into our relationship, as in the past, I was cold to his suggestion; however, she and I hit it off from the start and since then I have always found her fun to spend time with. I felt very comfortable around her and I was ready to take the relationship to the next level of intimacy. She quickly became our girlfriend and my first true same-sex relationship.

The beginning of our relationship with her was admittedly a little rough. I was nervous and I felt somewhat threatened. I still hadn't totally warmed up to this lifestyle yet and I was somewhat resentful. However, my perspective changed when he told me that she was attracted to <u>me</u>. I found myself looking at the situation differently. I realized that she wasn't being coerced and she had even suggested that the three of us become intimate. It seemed both weird and intriguing she was so interested in me. It definitely boosted my confidence and made me very excited about getting to know her better.

I don't totally remember how the evening of my first sexual encounter with her began. As I recall she came over for the evening, we had drinks, and my boyfriend was very flirtatious with both of us. The feeling was infectious and before long we were all in the bedroom. For sure I was nervous, there is no denying that but I quickly overcame it. She was so fun, so soft, and so attractive. We were very comfortable together, every movement and touch felt natural; it was also incredibly hot. She really turned me on, and it was one of the most pleasurable experiences of my life. Everyone gave equal time to the other and no one was left unsatisfied.

Before long she had moved into our apartment and became our first real girlfriend. There was definitely a period of adjustment. The traditional roles for a relationship didn't apply and we had to determine new boundaries. I felt that it was clear from the beginning she was the 'third' and that he and I had the primary relationship. I can't pretend to believe that it was easy for her either yet she was always very positive and loving. I also cannot pretend that the relationship was perfect. The low point for me was waking up one night to discover them having sex beside me. I felt disgusted and violated and openly expressed my loathing at their lack of respect. They quickly admitted their error and were remorseful of their decision; I was treated like a queen for the next few days while the hurt from their indiscretion faded.

It was so fun having a girlfriend **and** a boyfriend. It seemed to work so well, especially at dinner time when we shared the chores; everything just seemed easier. We loved hanging out at our apartment and we were totally open about our relationship with our growing circle of friends. Having a live-in girlfriend was good for me too; she had great style and liked to go dancing while my boyfriend often preferred to stay at home. I trusted her because I never perceived that she wanted to take my place. As such there was no jealously and the three of us made a strong triad.

She continued to live with us for several months, but then she moved on. I think that being a third is difficult especially in an established, long term relationship such as ours. She had a place in the relationship, but it was clear that it was not going to change. We had helped her at a time when she needed some support and some friendship. We had given her a place to live and a lot of love and she helped my boyfriend and I learn that we could successfully share our love. We had all benefited from the relationship equally. So when she told us she would be moving out, I was not upset; rather I understood her desire to move onto something more permanent.

My boyfriend took it harder than me because having a third was a bigger part of his identity than mine. He felt disappointed that she was breaking up with us while I was happy to return to our simple two person relationship. This and every "third" that came into our relationship afterwards had an impact. Some were positive and, unfortunately some were negative. I don't think I ever truly accepted that he preferred to have others in our relationship. I wanted him all to myself because I loved him so much. In retrospect I am thankful that he awoke my bisexuality and that I had the opportunity to experiment with alternative lifestyles. Today I am happy with monogamy and with my memories of past experiences.

After she moved out, she and I remained good friends. In times of distress she has always welcomed me to visit with her. I find her to be a comforting soul and wise despite her sometimes silly ways. She has listened to me when I have been upset and filled me with encouraging words. She continued to have lots of love for both of us after she moved on. She will forever hold a special place in my heart because she was the first girl with whom I was intimate. She opened my eyes to the beauty of women, and she also helped me to explore another facet of my personality.

In thinking about this first time I always make the same analogy in my mind. I compare having sex with a girl to jumping into a body of water. You stick your toes in and it feels cold, so you pull them away. You get warmed up and your courage builds so you try again but it's still cold. The more you look at the water the more inviting it becomes. Before long you can no longer resist the temptation and you just dive in. Then once you are in the water you realize how wonderful it is. You quickly feel relaxed and rejuvenated, you are happy with the experience, and look forward to doing it again. Sometimes you just have to jump in.

Feet First

Candace Clemens

Candace Clemens is the owner of Watson, a 16.2 hand Hanoverian dressage horse, and the mother of two grown daughters, ages 20 and 24. A bit of a rebel and an iconoclast, she regarded day-care as a liberating opportunity for her daughters to choose their neuroses cafeteria style, rather being condemned to perpetuating her own. As with the occasional rogue horse Candace has started under saddle, her daughters did their best to train their mother, but they finally gave up. Candace currently runs her own consulting firm: walnut28 communications, www.walnut28.com and has authored several annual reports and published articles in technology magazines: http://cclemens.typepad.com

We did the Lamaze classes, of course. I was finally ready to become a real woman. According to Lamaze, this happened ONLY if you experienced, start-to-finish, natural, vaginal childbirth, rejoicing in the pain of labor with each screaming contraction.

When I found out that my baby was standing up in my uterus (instead of on its head as was the norm), I was very concerned. I asked my doctor if there was anything I could do. He said that some women were able to get their fetuses to turn by elevating their lower torso slightly.

After thirty-two years, I was determined to become a real woman so I had to get my baby ready for natural childbirth. I asked if standing on my head might work even better than merely "elevating" my bottom over my top. Might the gravitational pull be more powerful? My doctor laughed…out loud. I thought I might be on to something. If it worked for me, I could spread the word to Lamaze teachers around the world.

It was night time in my living room. I was in my eighth month. Pregnancy wasn't fun anymore. It was uncomfortable. I was no longer glowing with the new life inside of me. Instead, my body was enormously deformed -- the incredible hulk painfully with child.

It had been many years since I had done a head-stand. I'm not sure how I managed just to get my head down on the floor, but I enlisted my husband's help in lifting my legs up over my head with the goal of propping my feet against the wall for stability.

However, each time he started to lift me, I imagined some passerby glancing through our bay window, only to see a huge, pregnant lady standing on her head. I burst out laughing, and my neck grew weak with laughter. I giggled hysterically, "Put me down, put me down." We tried a few more times, but once that giggle-producing thought creeps into your head, just like laughing in church, you can't get rid of it.

By the ninth month, I knew my baby was determined to land on its feet. I heard rumors that one of the women in my Lamaze class had a breeched baby. Hers was sideways. Much worse. But the danger of complications, such as the umbilical cord doing some damage was dramatically worse if the baby didn't come out head first. (Not to mention the pain of labor. But the latter didn't matter, as pain is part of the right of passage to "real" womanhood.)

What happened to her? I asked about my Lamaze peer. She had to go into emergency surgery. But in our small town hospital, there were only two operating rooms, and neither was available. I don't remember how this situation was resolved, but after hearing the story, I approached my doctor with great concern.

He suggested scheduling a C-Section. I wept. I was never going to become a woman. I probably wouldn't even be able to nurse my baby. The baby probably wouldn't even know who I was. I might as well just put my bundle of joylessness up for adoption if I couldn't deliver her naturally.

I called my brother-in-law, doctor of all doctors. He said that, in fact, surgery was the safest form of childbirth – for mother and child. The statistics were impressive. At this point I didn't stop to question. "Well, then, why all this fuss about Lamaze then? Why is everyone so obsessed with natural childbirth?" I was just relieved to know that, by opting for surgery, perhaps I was doing right by my baby. Maybe I could still become a mother and a "real woman."

So we scheduled our baby's delivery. Surgery was to be at 9:15 am on Feb. 3rd. I had to arrive at the hospital by 7 am, no food or water after midnight the night before.

I felt strange about this kind of birth. Where was the drama of the water breaking at an inopportune time? What about the strangely charming stories of birthing a healthy baby in a car in a snow storm? I wouldn't even be able to commiserate with other "real" women about the hours and days of horrible labor pains. This was so mundane. I felt like I was going to the grocery store to purchase a baby. I was being deprived of the greatest moment of my life! The moment that would make me a martyr for eternity, instilling healthy guilt in my husband and children.

They gave me a spinal which paralyzed me from the waist down. As they wheeled me on the gurney into the operating room reserved ahead of time just for my husband and me, I said to my husband Chris, "Wow, this is really pretty great. I think pain-free childbirth is really brilliant. If it's safer for mothers and babies, and there is little chance of emergencies, not to mention PAIN-FREE, why doesn't everybody do this?"

My stomach was a bit queasy, though. My doctor asked if I wanted to watch. The idea of watching him cut me open made me gag. So he put a little "curtain" up between my enormous belly and me. My husband held my hand, but peered around the curtain, watching the whole procedure.

A short time later, my doctor said, "I see some feet. I'm pulling them out. I see some legs. I see a bottom. And it is a little girl's bottom!" The doctor handed my baby to the nurse to weigh, and then asked my husband, now a dad, if he'd like to hold her. Chris jumped up and reported for duty with great enthusiasm. Then they took the baby away, and set about the job of sewing me up.

Chris stayed to watch this too. He asked, "What's that?"

"It's her uterus."

"You have to take it all the way out of her body?" Chris was incredulous.

"Yes. I have to sew it up. Then I put it back inside of her, and then I sew her up."

Already a bit squeamish, I was repulsed at the vision of one of my organs sitting outside of my body.

"Chris, would you SHUT UP?" I hissed through my teeth, hoping nobody on the other side of the curtain would hear me.

The doctor finished his job, and I was wheeled to the recovery room. On the gurney I was left facing the wall and a clock directly above my feet.

Then I started to realize why 'everybody' doesn't have a spinal.

It started as a headache and as the spinal wore off, my feet started jumping around with uncontrolled spasms. Everything hurt like hell. But most of all, the throbbing in my head was unbearable. Terrible pain. I felt like my head was going to explode.

"When can I get something for the pain?" I asked the nurse who stopped by to check my vital signs.

"When you get back to your hospital room," she answered crisply.

"How soon is that?" I responded quickly and plaintively.

"Oh in about twenty minutes," she said, as if that was no time at all.

I was there under the clock, watching the second hand move very slowly. I watched each minute go by, very, very slowly. My headache grew worse with each tick of the second hand, and the dancing feet continued to taunt me and my pain, asserting their independence from my body. Their argument with my brain over who owned their neurological impulses undoubtedly contributed to the excruciating headache.

After a very, very long time – for twenty minutes is quite long when you are counting the seconds for a much needed pain killer – my feet stopped dancing and they finally wheeled me out of that room. My throbbing, painful headache was worse than ever. I asked again, "Can I get something for the pain now?"

"We'll stop by the nursery first, so you can see your baby," the nurse said cheerily. "That should make you feel better."

GOD, LADY…THAT'S ALL I NEED FOR MY HEADACHE… A SCREAMING BABY. Somehow, I managed to keep from saying it out loud, but inside I was screaming it at the top of my lungs.

And so we stopped in front of the nursery. My mother-in-law first appeared in front of me just like that TUMS commercial, where all the relatives' faces appear distorted and enlarged in front of a fish eye lens, the eye of the afflicted. That was me and my headache. After the visage of my mother-in-law withdrew, a few other relatives loomed in front of me sequentially.

And then they brought this screaming baby over. My head was about to explode. Someone plopped her on my chest.

Instantly, the baby stopped crying. And instantly, my headache disappeared.

This was the first of many child-related experiences I was to have that reminded me that underneath all the layers of education and civilization, we are merely mammals. Our bodies are filled with instincts, bodily processes, chemicals, bio-chemical and biological reactions that are way beyond our control. Unless we study them, we have no knowledge about how powerful these instincts and biological drives are. We are not much different than salmon swimming upstream. Our bodies are driving us to do a job before we die. And so we do it.

With my second child, I went through twenty hours of labor, the first contraction as painful as the one I had just before they put me on an epidural. Ahhhh, epidurals -- God's true gift to women.

Lamaze classes should be renamed Epidural Classes. In fact, as the years of motherhood unfolded, as the challenges of life forged a "real woman," I came to wish there was an epidural for life.

Green

Nathan Cutler

Nathan's entire childhood was spent in the fishing village of Ramea. He is married with three grown children and returns with his wife most summers for a visit to his native province of Newfoundland.

All too fast the three weeks of our vacation had flown by. The much anticipated holiday had been planned since last year. This was the summer my twin brother and I would visit my cousins, Aunt Mary, and Uncle Lee on the west coast of Newfoundland.

We had visited once before when I was eleven with my mom and the six of us kids. This time it was just the two of us. We were thirteen and could be counted on to behave while traveling on the coastal steamer for two days and then a six hour train ride. We traveled under the watchful eye of one of mom's friends who also lived in our little out-port fishing town and who was also traveling to the same west-coast city. There was no question of behavior of the highest standard as it would secure visits sometime again in those long summers to come.

Now on this first morning back home, I pushed away from the breakfast table walking towards the door.

"Where are you going?" called Mom.

I wasn't sure, but maybe up the road to play cowboys and Indians with the best friends or whatever it was they were playing since we had left. No doubt the newest take of the latest Saturday matinee they watched while we were away.

Stepping outside into the sunshine I have no idea why the glistening, silvery sparkles caught my attention. The reflection bounced from the thin pathway that ran directly beneath the clothesline where my mother had just propped up the latest batch of laundry, with a long thin pole, to dry in the morning sun. The grass blades all bent in the direction of her footsteps as she had reached up and pinned the individual pieces of clothing to the line. Now the occasional breeze caught them causing the clothing to flutter in the wind their moisture lost to the sun's warm rays. The excess water dripped onto the grass below, caressing and trickling down the blade's curved backs, the tiny droplets disappearing into the ground as if knowing it was their rightful place.

Aunt Mary never hung her clothing outside: she had a dryer. Her and Uncle Lee's house was much like ours but oh so much bigger and filled with appliances, new stylish furniture, and carpets. They had an electric stove and even some of the meals were different from what I was used to, like the delicious chicken baked in BBQ sauce. We always had gravy at home and although tasty, I preferred Aunt Mary's red sauce over Mom's brown gravy.

For a moment I heard Aunt Mary asking, "What are you staring at?" as I absorbed the huge expanse of golf course that nearly encircled their house and garden.

"Oh nothing," I replied as I studied the small electric vehicles that carried people holding what looked like hockey sticks minus the blades. Boys my age lugged large long leather knapsacks tossing what looked like snowballs. The course was made up of evenly spaced shiny green patches that resembled the softest carpet I had ever seen. Adults, striding with purpose, took much time hitting the small white objects towards holes dug in the center of each green. I wondered how the grass here was kept so short as I saw no sheep and the fields seemed to roll on forever into the horizon.

The whole expanse was as large as the out-port where I had grown up. Uncle Lee oversaw this operation, sort of like back home where dad ran a ship and its crew. This appeared so much nicer than home, I thought; I tried to dismiss the feelings of envy towards my cousins. Of course I knew I could never express these feelings, to do so was not kind.

I turned to ask Aunt Mary a question, but realized I was now looking back at my own door. Aunt Mary and Uncle Lee's place was so much what I would like as my home. From the first day of our arrival to live in their house and the ensuing three weeks, my time was filled with indescribable delights along with the wonderment of city living.

Now as I walked along the narrow path under Mom's clothesline I felt pulled as if by some cosmic magic to check out the sparkle of the dripping water as it struck home onto the blades of bent grass. Beyond the grass ran our fence that until a few years ago seemed a mile high as I recalled desperately attempting time and time again to climb up and over. A feat accomplished in my ninth year. Oh to master that six foot high wall and run into the next garden.

Next door's garden was where my mother often sent us with a small picnic basket filled with crackers, a few rice-crispy squares, and a container of lime juice, the smell of which I recall to this day. If we were lucky we were even given a can of Vienna sausages. For major picnics there were more goodies. As we all sat on that special picnic blanket breathing in the fresh clean air of out-port life each picnic item was savored as if it were Christmas morning.

Today, however, I was back home and already the summer holidays seemed as but a dream and everything seemed less bright and crisp. I bent to take a closer look at the gem-like sparkles on the wet grass.

In doing so I was overwhelmed.

For ever so brief a moment, I was transported to a higher level. The world stopped for a moment, the sky grew a deep blue, the robin on the clothes pole sang more beautifully, the gentle breeze on my face was just that – gentle, and through the sparkling diamond-like moisture on the blades of uncut grass I saw the color green. A green so brilliant, vibrant, and clear that it caught my breath and for the first time I saw the Universe right here in my own backyard on this side of the fence. The Universe shining in the tiny beads of water on each bent leaf of uncut grass and trickling into the roots as if saying I'm home.

The Week I Died
Chuck Duncan

Chuck Duncan is an engineer and inventor who wrote a monthly column called "Ask Dr. Microsoft" in a corporate, world-wide newsletter for a Fortune 100 company. His passion is writing action, adventure novels and his first full-length book titled 'Sleight of Hand' is nearing publication. He is currently hard at work on a sequel.

I lie cold and alone, a world away from home in a jungle in Southeast Asia, a place I wasn't supposed to be, a time that was the wrong time. I'm supposed to be at home going out with my girlfriend who promised to wait for me, and whose picture sits frayed and wrinkled in my pocket, a bullet hole in one corner, my blood soaking it as I stare into the dark sky partially masked by trees waving in the gentle breeze. It fades from sight along with the pain, and I drift off like it was all a bad dream. The world disappears from sight once more.

~~~~~~

The ground is hard and cold, and my eyes begin to focus once more.

I'm still here. Damn! I thought I would have been gone by now. What will it be like this time? Will I continue to suffer? After all I have gone through I don't care what the outcome is as long as it ends.

I am burning up with fever in the cold night air as though I'm standing in a blast furnace. I would sweat if my body had an ounce of water left amongst the strained muscle fibers.

I stare into the darkness alone my body limp and lifeless with only flickering remnants of a soul. I can see clearly again. It's night. I have gone through days and nights, just lying here, how many, I lost track a long time ago. I'm stuck in an endless cycle of misery.

I am slowly cooling off now. I know I am not getting better though each time I wake, I grasp for remaining morsels of hope like digging for seeds in quicksand. Each time I try, I am overtaken again and cast into a depth of darkness.

I know I am dying – slowly and surely. I won't let go. I won't give up. I am not beaten until I become unconscious that last time. A brave young man entered this land, and here I lie scared, lost, and alone. I had just assumed that when I died it would be among friends, family, in a familiar place, but I am being robbed of such a gift. Mine is the agony of a slow and miserable demise.

My body finally cools down and comes to rest. I cling to this moment of peace as my only friend – a strand of connection to life, my breathing shallow. My fingers touch the dry leaves beneath my hands, and I think of how they once were born of a tree, grew, flourished, and then came to lay on the ground beneath me their entire existence destined to form a casket around my body. They followed the same path from birth, through life, and now join me in death – both of us "from dust to dust."

I haven't had food or water for almost a week. I tried to sip water days ago, just to go into endless vomiting like a shit-faced teenager who, drunk out of his mind, now pays the price. Now I can only lie still in one spot lacking the strength to move.

I relish this moment of peace. I pray to my God. I remember Jesus' words on the cross: "My God, My God, Why hast though forsaken me." I have no right to utter these words, but I do with simple remorse. Why must I suffer this? What have I to gain from facing this Hell? I love my God – even in this terrible moment; I just don't understand.

A shiver races the length of my body signaling the start of another trip through Hell. I am focusing on the shiver, hoping I can control it and prevent another from following. It fades for a brief moment and then another emerges, and soon another, and another, and I begin to freeze and shake violently. If I had enough strength, I would be convulsing. I begin to choke in mock vomiting. I lost all stomach contents days ago, and now I am only left with choking and gasping for air that comes reluctantly and never satisfies my desire for life.

The world begins to swirl around me like being strapped to one of those carnival rides that disorients by random gyrations in three-dimensions. The fear descends upon me like a flood of black oil. My eyes fail to capture even the faintest image, and I fear that I will somehow be thrown about and injure myself further. I have to get my bearings. With my outstretched arms, I press my hands onto the ground focusing on the palms and the heels of my feet in a belief that they will convince me that I am not moving. The vertigo spins faster and faster and -- darkness -- emptiness -- floating -- silence.

It will be a long time before I awaken again burning up with a fever that consumes remaining morsels of energy within me. A rescuer could have walked over me, and I wouldn't have known it. The cycle repeats. I didn't die that time. Maybe next time.

But wait! There is a sound in the distance - a voice I think. Is it real or just an illusion? I have no voice with which to answer. I hold my breath so I can hear better. There it is again.

I have to move. Somehow I must summon the last of my strength. I manage to roll over onto my stomach, my face presses against the cold ground. I lie still gasping until I catch my breath, and then I try to move again.

There it is again -- the voice -- it is real. I claw at the ground and drag myself toward the sound. I have to move now before I pass out again. My feet push as my fingers dig into the ground for a better grip. I summon movement from a body that long since lost hope of functioning, and it rebels against my torturous demands, but each movement brings me closer to the sound.

I shiver and shake. I can't stop now or I will miss the voice; I won't be rescued. My muscles have no strength, and the dim light passes.

A long time has passed and I awaken face down. I have only gone thirty or forty feet. Is it luck or divine intervention that has brought the voices closer? I cannot take time to fully regain consciousness. Now is the time to try again. I claw and push, claw and push, until I begin to fall. Voices are rushing up to me, but so is a roar like Niagara Falls. The roar blocks my hearing. I am gone again. Did I make it in time? Will I come back again, or have I simply delivered my body to the place of my burial.

It can't end here. I have to know that someone found me – dead or alive – they must find me here. I can't die yet. The girlfriend waiting at home will never know what happened to me. She will be dragged through the same Hell I have gone through, waiting to receive word, hoping, praying in vain, looking into the darkness for the light to come just as I have – a light that never comes -- being caught in an endless cycle of pain until her love finally dies. If we must die, we deserve to do so quickly, but this has not been granted to me. I beg of my God, don't make her go through the pain that I have. Let me bear that pain for both of us.

Darkness pursues me, and the roar fades into silence.

~~~~~~~

I wish I could say the first time I almost died seems like a long time ago, but it doesn't. Such trauma is not easily forgotten. Simple things bring back a terror that cannot be described. I shiver from a cold draft and drop to the floor. The sound of rustling leaves in a soft breeze bring forth uncontrolled vomiting. How many times have these events brought only pleasure; then why should I only remember pain?

Today, the sun shines brightly. I am at the high point of my life after having once visited the depths of Hell. Where before I bathed in darkness and fear, I now bask in light and love.

How vibrant this new life is. Was this my reward for facing death and not giving in? Would I have fully appreciated each instant of love as deeply had I not struggled so to come back and achieve it? My wife – the girl who waited at home for my return -- understands my deep passion for her, but may never fully understand how important each second is to me, how desperately I cling to the joy of the moment, my commitment to feeling love and happiness. I still have that worn and stained photo of her locked away somewhere because it reminds me that it was the love we shared that kept me alive, that fueled my soul, and brought me home.

They say that birth is more traumatic than death. I think not. I have been through both. Perhaps it was not death I experienced, but a second birth – a birth of the spirit. It may be a long time before I fully understand the why of my life.

I sit on the porch swing in the evening holding my wife's hand in mine as we look out on a golden sunset through the trees, feel the gentle wind, and revel in the brilliant colors that adorn the passion of our love. It was worth it – every moment – and knowing what I know now, knowing the love that is mine, for her, I would do it all again.

A Writer's Confessional

Jennifer Cutler

Jennifer currently lives in Massachusetts with her husband and daughter. Hiking, walking, writing, and play-dates have become a way of life and much to Jennifer's surprise, quite an enjoyable one.

I write from the male perspective. When my husband pointed out this particular quirk, I shook my head at how something so unusual had escaped my attention for over two years. On top of that, it didn't really make sense. I'm what one might consider a woman of the traditional female persuasion: I enjoy nothing more than chit-chatting with girlfriends over coffee, shedding tears over stories about lost love and inner journeys, and I take great pride in my ability to nurture dying plants back to life.

Yet every protagonist in every story I've written is a man: a rough and tumble loner whose idea of romance often includes unbridled treachery and manipulation. Outside of the romance department, they are heroes and I love them for that. I understand what makes them tick. Our inevitable friendship grows over a series of months as I sit down with them for a couple hours each day sculpting away the rubbish until the character, the man emerges. There have been weeks I've spent more time with my latest hero than my husband.

My gang of men are similar to each other in some respects. They are a good sort and I'd like to think they'd be friendly with each other if they met at a party. That is, as long as no one drank too much: a couple of them don't know when to call it a night. Each of them has a magnetic personality, an underlying confidence, and every one of them is ready to play the champion when the occasion arises.

They have their differences too. Humphrey is a private detective, Maxwell is a home-sick rig-worker, Dexter and Hayden are both aficionados of overseas travel, but Dexter is an intellectual and Hayden is nothing more than a cultural imperialist. Thomas is an addicted gambler trying to dig his family out of debt no matter the cost and Sal - well, Sal is an immigrant teenager who is learning to watch out for his own best interests in the midst of all that Santa Cruz peer pressure. Helix lives in Nevada and James in Quincy. They're all problem-solvers who mine deep reserves of energy and intellect in times of crisis. Even if panicked waves of nauseating fear rise to scare them off, it's only momentary and eventually they deal with the situation courageously, always coming out ahead even if it's on their own terms. All but chain-smoking Thomas; for some reason he didn't rise to the occasion, and in the end he gets what he deserves.

So at this revelation over supper that all my main characters are male, my mind wandered towards two stories hidden at the back of my bedroom closet. I tucked them away soon after they were written. My husband hasn't read them. In fact, no one has. Both stories are led by women whom I've protected as a priest does his confessional flock.

So the next morning when I was alone, I pulled out the two stories and reread them to be promptly struck by an epiphany, but I'll get to that in a moment.

These two ladies whom I've never taken the time to really get to know aren't gentlewomen. They're rough and socially awkward. They tend to over-think, paranoia guiding their self-analysis as they nit-pick yesterday's events with an irritating and repetitive worry. Neither Mary nor Ceebee would stand out at a party, unless someone was really into red-heads, and Ceebee would just recoil from the attention anyway.

Both women struggle alone and in their weakest moments, some may label them clinically depressed. In 'One Monday Morning' we stumble upon Mary. She's emotionally fragile and focuses on the problems in her life, not the possible solutions. Her choices just perpetuate her numb existence.

Ceebee Joy, whom I follow through 'The Proverbial Pope', is at least more admirable. She's a professional whose cynicism and artistic nature enable her success as a photographer for a mid-sized Ontario newspaper, the Hamilton Sun. She likes to think of herself as hopeful and fun-loving, but in the company of others, she gives the impression of being a bit too serious and somewhat of a kill-joy at times. I like her much more than old Mary pining away in her little cottage perched on the cliffs of Nova Scotia's coastline. Thankfully, Ceebee reaches life-changing conclusions by the end of the story even if she had to crawl through misery to reach them.

It was painful to read the first story, the one about Mary. 'In the distance, thunder rolled across the ocean and dark, endless storm clouds marched towards him. His unfocused eyes watched the grey sea, the rolling sky. To him, it looked as though the sea was heaving blood.' Mary's abandonment of her newborn son strikes a low tone deep in my heart. I despise her for it and what's worse she blames others for her decision. A sickening resonance filled my stomach and as I read the last paragraph, I grimaced, recoiling visibly. My reaction surprised me.

Then I picked up Ceebee's story. It was reading this story that drew me closer to my epiphany. In it, I glimpsed something chilling, bothersome, familiar like a long-forgotten secret that rises through the murky waters of time to surface with undeniable certainty.

I realized for the first time Ceebee and Mary were Me. The two women represent my yin: death on a winter's night, a watery, cold moon, the hidden darkness of my id that haunts me when I am alone. And there it sat in cold-blood in Ceebee's story: Chapter eleven, page two, paragraph six: 'She preferred the anger scenario; his indifference would cripple her, and guilt would breed even more hatred for herself.'

Of course as I was writing this story I realized I was drawing on my own experiences, but guilt and hatred? This was news to me. My mind reeled as I attempted to hold onto an internal railing to steady myself. Had Ceebee been created not by my conscious mind but by my mutinous moralistic super-ego? In that chapter, Ceebee is reflecting on her secret: a red-haired child she placed for adoption ten years prior. Just like I did.

Ceebee and I shared that dreadful moment of stomach-twisting panic, an unspeakable grief when we placed our first-born sons in other women's arms. Walking away from the hospital to begin life 'without baby'; the conception nurtured and adored for nine months now gone was misery shared with Ceebee.

Two days old, now three, now a week, we obsessed over the decision. The future was bleak: no money, no familial-support, no long-term plans, but maybe just maybe the local YMCA rented car-seats. Maybe Ceebee could go get her son. Perhaps I could find my own apartment and raise him, even if it meant social assistance and working part-time.

I knew how Ceebee felt ten years later as she thought back on that hell. The first month post-adoption was nothing but spiraling thoughts, no answers, only questions. Did her little boy wonder where his mommy was? Did he feel abandoned? When he cried, was it for her, her smell, her voice, her touch? As she leaked milk her child cried hundreds of miles away from her breast and she asked herself if she was a monster. She lay comatose staring into the rawness, her heart irreparably cracked.

But in the end, Ceebee was a hero, just like my guys, and she signed the papers. Following were months of sadness and years of melancholy. And now ten years later, right there on the page, Ceebee still tortured herself jabbing herself with self-reproach and guilt at what she'd done.

So to read about these lingering doubts shocked me.

I had risen from the ashes. And I moved on eventually meeting the right man and fulfilling my dream of bringing home a baby to love and nurture. So when I saw Ceebee's pain, I realized for the first time, how hard the adoption had really been, how the scars only partially heal, no matter the lapse of time; when a child is lost, a decade is a snap of the fingers.

My discovery of writing and its release was realized at a young age; about the age my biological son is now. I hope as he nears adulthood, he discovers his own way to liberate his feelings on his journey through life's valleys and its breath-taking peaks. And I pray when he does find himself alone and in pain, self-torture is never the path he chooses.

Self-discovery, accepting choices and regret, forgoing blame and taking responsibility all tie into an incredible story of love; Ceebee did what she could for her son. After the adoption, she suffered, she ran, and eventually she reached the end of the road with nowhere else to look but inward.

Ceebee is a friend I protect and she, like my gang of guys, stand in my way until I liberate them from their suffering. And when I do, they return the favor.

www.ingramcontent.com/pod-product-compliance
Ingram Content Group UK Ltd.
Pitfield, Milton Keynes, MK11 3LW, UK
UKHW050411240426
12048UKWH00020B/1453